Original text by Jane Shaw
Updated by Sally Roy

© Automobile Association Developments Limited 2009
First published 2007
Reprinted 2009. Information verified and updated

ISBN: 978-0-7495-6012-6

Published by AA Publishing, a trading name of Automobile Association Developments
Limited, whose registered office is Fanum House, Basing View, Basingstoke,
Hampshire RG21 4EA. Registered number 1878835.

Colour separation: MRM Graphics Ltd
Printed and bound in Italy by Printer Trento S.r.l.

A03616
Maps in this title produced from mapping © MAIRDUMONT / Falk Verlag 2008
Transport map © Communicarta Ltd, UK

About this book

Symbols are used to denote the following categories:

➕ map reference to maps on cover
✉ address or location
☎ telephone number
🕓 opening times
✋ admission charge
🍴 restaurant or café on premises or nearby
🚇 nearest underground train station
🚌 nearest bus/tram route
🚃 nearest overground train station
⛴ nearest ferry stop
✈ nearest airport
ℹ tourist information office
❓ other practical information
➤ indicates the page where you will find a fuller description

This book is divided into five sections.

The essence of Italy pages 6–19
Introduction; Features; Food and drink; Short break including the 10 Essentials

Planning pages 20–33
Before you go; Getting there; Getting around; Being there

Best places to see pages 34–55
The unmissable highlights of any visit to Italy

Best things to do pages 56–75
Good places to have lunch; stunning views; great beaches; best frescoes; places to take the children; places to stay and more

Exploring pages 76–187
The best places to visit in Italy, organized by area

Maps
All map references are to the maps on the covers. For example, Ravenna has the reference ➕ 6D – indicating the grid square in which it is to be found.

Admission prices
Inexpensive (under €5);
Moderate (€5–€8);
Expensive (over €8)

Hotel prices
Price are per room per night:
€ budget (under €150);
€€ moderate (€150–€250);
€€€ expensive to luxury (over €250)

Restaurant prices
Price for a three-course meal per person without drinks:
€ budget (under €30);
€€ moderate (€30–€50);
€€€ expensive (over €50)

Contents

BEST THINGS TO DO

EXPLORING...

56 – 75   76 – 186

The essence of...

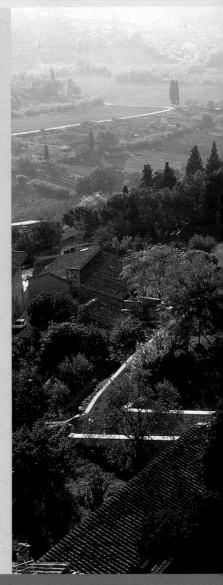

Italy has one of the oldest tourist industries in the world, having been among the principal destinations for the rich 'grand tourists' in the 18th and 19th centuries. They came here to sample the ancient, Renaissance and baroque delights of Venice, Florence and Tuscany, Rome, Naples and (for the more adventurous) Sicily. These places still have an enormous pull, but unless you are really short of time, don't limit yourself to mainstream tourist Italy. Almost anywhere is within reach of little towns and villages, isolated ancient remains, mountains or the sea, so make the most of these delights for a richly varied stay in one of the world's most beautiful countries.

features

Yes, Italy is full of stunning towns and cities full of unbelievably beautiful buildings and populated by attractive, friendly people whose musical language makes the most banal of observations sound poetic (until you understand them), but the life that is going on is just as real as it is in any other European country. Sure, things don't always work the way you would like them to, and you may spend half a day paying a cheque into your bank account or queuing up in some state office to tackle the complex bureaucracy. But a lot of this is improving, and Italy is more efficient and streamlined than ever before.

Even if you are only here for a few days, you are likely to have several surprises – some good and some bad. Be flexible, relax and you can't go wrong; the museum you have gone out of your way to see may be shut when it should be open, but

instead you might end up having a memorable lunch in a restaurant where, after the coffee, the proprietor plies you with some ambrosian *digestivo* made with fruit from his own orchard.

THE COUNTRY

Italy covers a famously boot-shaped area of land stretching for around 1,300km (810 miles) from the Alps in the north to Sicily, level with the northern tip of Africa, in the south. About 25 per cent of this area consists of plains (such as that of the River Po) and the rest is hilly or mountainous. There are 7,600km (4,723 miles) of coastline.

THE PEOPLE

Just over 50 per cent of the 58 million or so people living in Italy today live in towns of at least 20,000 inhabitants. Until Unification in 1870, the Italian nation did not exist; the country was divided into several small states, each with its own history and culture. Regionalism is still strong throughout Italy and not just at the level of cuisine and dialect; each of the 20 regions has a degree of political autonomy.

ECONOMY

Since World War II Italy has found itself among the top ten world economic powers, although most of this wealth is in the north. Its main agricultural crops include olives, grapes, wheat, rice and tomatoes, and among its main industries are motor vehicles, domestic appliances, fashion, pasta and tourism.

One of the side affects of Italy's economic boom has been the reversal of emigration habits. Until 1974 Italy exported workers; since then (and particularly since the late 1980s), the outward flow has turned into an influx of immigrants, particularly from northern Africa, eastern Europe, the Philippines and the USA, and now there are more than 1.2 million foreigners registered as residents in Italy, as well as tens of thousands of illegal immigrants from eastern Europe and North Africa.

food & drink

Italians are justly proud of their cuisine, which is among the finest and (according to research) the most healthy in the world. Although certain staples can be found all over the country, each region has its own specialities, based on history, tradition and the best of local produce.

PRIMI (FIRST COURSES)

Pasta comes in a wide variety of shapes and with every imaginable accompanying sauce (*condimento*). *Spaghetti alle vongole* (with clams) can be found in most coastal regions. *Pesto* – chopped basil, olive oil, Parmesan cheese and pine nuts – is a Ligurian speciality, while *ragù* (meat sauce) is common in central Italy, *carbonara* (bacon, eggs and pecorino cheese) in Rome, and pasta with sardines in Sicily. Rice is often used in place of pasta, especially in the north near the Po Valley, where it is grown. It is used in dishes such as

risotto alla Milanese and with black squid ink in Venice (and also Sicily). Polenta is another particularly northern alternative to pasta; a thick, porridge-like or even solid substance made from ground maize.

SECONDI (MAIN COURSES)

Veal *(vitello)* and chicken *(pollo)* are common throughout Italy. Lamb *(agnello)* is more common in south central and southern Italy, while beef *(manzo)* is used in the north. In Abruzzo, goat is a speciality, especially in spring, and wild boar *(cingliale)* appears on many north central menus.

Wide use is made in many areas of offal (liver, kidneys, heart and even brains and intestines) and horsemeat (or donkey in Sardinia), famed for its high iron and low fat content. Fish and seafood include sardines, mussels, clams, tuna and swordfish (the last two particularly in the south), while lakeside areas make good use of freshwater fish and eels.

CONTORNI (VEGETABLES)

A wide variety of mushrooms (including the popular *funghi porcini)* comes in particular from central Italy where, together with truffles, they are gathered wild during spring and autumn. Rocket (arugula) leaves are used in salads and with cold meats, while deep-fried courgette (zucchini) flowers, in batter with a hint of anchovy and cheese, are a common *antipasto* option. The Rome area is famous for artichokes, while the best tomatoes come from Calabria.

DOLCI (DESSERTS)

Apart from the ubiquitous *tiramisù* and *gelati*, you'll be tempted by such delights as *torta alla ricotta* in the south and south central regions;

cantucci (hard almond biscuits) served with sweet *vin santo* for dunking in Tuscany, and light, spongy *panettone*, a Milanese speciality.

WINES AND DRINKS

Almost anywhere you go in Italy, the basic wines served as house wine in restaurants range from reliably drinkable to good. Top-quality reds come from Piedmont (Barolo, Dolcetto and Barbera d'Alba) and Tuscany (Vino Nobile di Montepulciano, Brunello di Montalcino

and Chianti Classico). The best of the whites and sparkling wines include still Pinot Grigio and lightly sparkling Prosecco from the northeast, sparkling Moscato d'Asti from the northwest, and still Orvieto Classico from Umbria. Marsala and dessert wines are a particular Sicilian speciality.

The massive list of drinks to stimulate your appetite *(aperitivi)* includes Campari and Martini, while, to help you digest, *digestivi* include grappas that range from firewater to silky smooth, and *amari* – thick, sticky concoctions made with herbs.

short break

If you only have a short time to visit Italy and would like to take home some unforgettable memories you can do something local and capture the real flavour of the country. The following suggestions will give you a wide range of experiences that won't take very long, won't cost very much and will make your visit very special.

● **Enjoy the art:** select a few of Italy's artists and notice the variety and geographical spread of the works that each has left.

● **Spend at least half a day** without a map or guidebook in the historic centre of a city or large town, and just soak up the atmosphere.

- **Spend a whole afternoon over lunch** in typical Italian style and slip into a more relaxed pace of life.

- **Visit at least one ancient site,** even if it's just a Roman amphitheatre. There is bound to be one within reach of where you are staying.

- **Attend an outdoor play,** opera or concert – an enchanting experience in Italy's generally benign climate.

- **Spend a day on the beach;** rent an umbrella and sun-bed and watch the world go by.

● **Eat ice cream** wherever you go and compare the types and quality. The variety of flavours will astonish you.

● **See some mountains or lakes** and enjoy a bit of the outdoor life. There is some spectacular scenery in Italy, from the Alpine region and Italian Lakes in the north to the central backbone of the Appenines and volcanic peaks in the south.

● **Take a trip to an island:** some, like Capri (➤ 176), are beautiful but busy tourist hot spots, while others offer peace and quiet off the beaten track.

● **Visit at least one of the smaller towns:** many contain architectural treasures to compare with those of the great cities, and have a timeless ambience all their own.

Planning

Before you go

WHEN TO GO

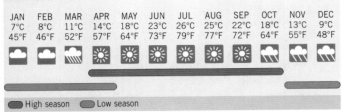

	JAN	FEB	MAR	APR	MAY	JUN	JUL	AUG	SEP	OCT	NOV	DEC
	7°C	8°C	11°C	14°C	18°C	23°C	26°C	25°C	22°C	18°C	13°C	9°C
	45°F	46°F	52°F	57°F	64°F	73°F	79°F	77°F	72°F	64°F	55°F	48°F

🔴 High season   🟠 Low season

Italy's climate ranges from Alpine in the mountains of the far north and scorching hot and dry in the most southerly areas. The central section is more variable, with summer temperatures often exceeding 30°C (86°F) and consistent sunshine during the day. The hottest months are July to September, and at this time humidity is boosted by the hot Sirocco wind blowing up from Africa. Overnight temperatures can also be very high, and city residents (particularly Romans) tend to head for the coast and countryside.

In winter, the north becomes a winter-sports playground, while the rest of the country – even the south – is often plagued by rain and fog and can be bitterly cold. Venice is prone to flooding, and so are some other areas.

WHAT YOU NEED

		UK	Germany	USA	Netherlands	Spain
● Required	Some countries require a passport to remain valid for a minimum period (usually at least six months) beyond the date of entry – contact their consulate or embassy or your travel agent for details.					
○ Suggested						
▲ Not required						
Passport (or National Identity Card where applicable)		●	●	●	●	▲
Visa (regulations can change – check before you travel)		▲	▲	▲	▲	▲
Onward or Return Ticket		▲	▲	▲	▲	▲
Health Inoculations (tetanus and polio)		▲	▲	▲	▲	▲
Health Documentation (► 23, Health Advice)		●	●	▲	●	●
Travel Insurance		○	○	○	○	○
Driving Licence (national)		●	●	●	●	●
Car Insurance Certificate		●	●	●	●	●
Car Registration Document		●	●	●	●	●

WEBSITES

- www.enit.it (the site of the Italian State Tourist Office)
- www.italiantourism.com (a site especially for visitors from the US)
- www.romaturismo.it (the website of the Rome tourist office)
- www.museionline.it (the official site for state and other museums across Italy
- www.firenze.net (the best Florence website)
- www.trenitalia.it (for booking Italy's excellent rail system)

TOURIST OFFICES AT HOME

In the UK

Italian State Tourist Board
✉ 1 Princes Street, London W1B 8AY ☎ 020 7408 1254;
www.enit.it

In the USA

Italian State Tourist Board
✉ 630 Fifth Avenue, Suite 1565, New York NY 10111
☎ 212/245-5618;
www.italiantourism.com

Italian State Tourist Board
✉ 12400 Wilshire Boulevard Suite 550, Los Angeles CA 90025
☎ 310/820-1898;
www.italiantourism.com

HEALTH ADVICE

Insurance Nationals of EU countries receive reduced cost medical and dental treatment within the Italian health service and pay a percentage for prescribed medicines. You need a European Health Insurance Card (EHIC). Private medical insurance is still advised. US visitors should check their insurance coverage.

TIME DIFFERENCES

| GMT | Italy | Germany | USA (NY) | Netherlands | Spain |
| 12 noon | 1PM | 1PM | 7AM | 1PM | 1PM |

Italy is one hour ahead of Greenwich Mean Time (GMT+1), but from late March, when clocks are put forward one hour, to late October, Italian Summer Time (GMT+2) operates.

NATIONAL HOLIDAYS

1 January *New Year's Day*
6 January *Epiphany*
March/April *Easter Monday*
25 April *Liberation Day, 1945*
1 May *Labour Day*
15 August *Assumption of the Virgin*

1 November *All Saints' Day*
8 December *Immaculate Conception*
25 December *Christmas Day*
26 December *St Stephen's Day*

Banks, businesses and most shops and museums close on these days. Most cities, towns and villages celebrate their patron saint's day, but generally, most places remain open.

WHAT'S ON WHEN

Saints' Days The events listed below are only a few of the traditional holidays and feast days that are celebrated in Italy. Most communities also have religious parades on their patron saint's day, when effigies and relics of the saint and/or Virgin are taken in procession from the main church and paraded through the streets by priests, nuns, monks and pilgrims, often in historic costume. They usually finish at some significant spot (often in or by the sea in coastal communities) and are followed by general celebrations.

January *New Year's Day:* public holiday.
Epiphany (6 Jan): public holiday. Traditionally the *befana* (witch) leaves presents for children.

February Week leading up to Shrove Tuesday: *Carnevale*. Streets full of adults and children in fancy dress throwing confetti and firecrackers. Particularly important in Venice.

March/April *Good Friday:* Pope leads ceremony of the Stations of the Cross at the Colosseum in Rome (► 44–45).
Easter Sunday: Papal address from San Pietro (► 36–37).
Settimana Beni Culturali (Late Mar–early Apr): a week of free admission

and guided tours to state museums and other, infrequently open, monuments.

Rome's birthday (21 Apr): music all over the city and fireworks at night.

Liberation Day (25 Apr): public holiday. Commemorates the Allies' liberation of Italy from the Nazis in 1944.

Maggio Musicale Fiorentino, Firenze (late Apr): Classical music, dance and opera festival, featuring world-class performers and conductors.

May *Labour Day* (1 May): public holiday.

Festa dei Ceri, Gubbio (5 May): (➤ 134–135).

June *Calcio Storico Fiorentino* (24 Jun): costume procession, fireworks and a ball game in Piazza della Signoria, Florence.

July/August

Palio, Siena (2 Jul): Costumed participants take part in flag-waving and a fearsome bareback horse-race round Piazza del Campo.

Opera at the Terme di Caracalla in Rome (beginning Jul to mid-Aug): Spectacularly big outdoor productions of popular operas in the ruins of the Baths of Caracalla, often featuring huge choruses and live animals.

August *Ferragosto* (15 Aug): public holiday. Many businesses close for a week or more.

Palio (16 Aug): see 2 July.

Giostra del Saracino, Arezzo (last Sun in Aug): medieval joust.

September *Regata Storica*, Venice (first Sun in Sep): a colourful procession of historic boats and a gondola race.

November *All Saints' Day* (1 Nov): public holiday.

December *Immaculate Conception* (8 Dec): public holiday.

Christmas Day (25 Dec): public holiday. Papal address at San Pietro (➤ 36–37).

New Year's Eve (31 Dec): fireworks, free concerts and massive *cenone* (dinners) in many restaurants.

Getting there

BY AIR

Leonardo da Vinci (Fiumicino)

32km (20 miles) to city centre

🚆 30–45 minutes
🚌 50 minutes
🚗 40 minutes

Ciampino Airport

15km (9 miles) to city centre

🚆 N/A
🚌 55 minutes
🚗 30–45 minutes

Internazionale Linate

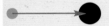

7km (4 miles) to city centre

🚆 N/A
🚌 30–40 minutes
🚗 15 minutes

Intercontinentale della Malpensa

50km (31 miles) to city centre

🚆 40 minutes
🚌 45–60 minutes
🚗 35–60 minutes

Marco Polo Airport

12km (7.5 miles) to city centre

🚆 N/A
🚌 20 minutes
🚗 15–25 minutes

Galileo Galilei Airport

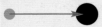

91km (57 miles) to city centre

🚆 10 minutes
🚌 10 minutes
🚗 5 minutes

There are direct flights from Europe and North America to Italy's major
international airports.

Rome's main airport is Leonardo da Vinci, or Fiumicino (tel: 06 65 951; www.adr.it), which is 32km (20 miles) from central Rome. It takes 30–45 minutes by the express rail service to Stazione Termini. The other airport serving Rome is Ciampino (tel: 06 65951; www.adr.it), 15km (9 miles) to the southeast. The journey by car takes 40–50 minutes, and a bus link operates throughout the day.

Internazionale Linate and Intercontinentale della Malpensa airports both serve Milan (tel: 02 7485 2200; www.sea-aeroportimilano.it). Linate is 7km (4 miles) from central Milan. Malpensa airport is 50km (31 miles) northwest of Milan, 40 minutes by train from Milano Nord station.

Venice's Marco Polo Airport (tel: 041 260 9260; www.veniceairport.it) is 7km (4 miles) from the city by boat across the lagoon, or 12km (7.5 miles) by road. Water taxis get you to the city in 20–35 minutes, land taxis to Piazzale Roma take 15–25 minutes.

Florence and Pisa are served by Galileo Galilei Airport (tel: 050 849300; www.pisa-airport.com), in Pisa, 91km (57 miles) west of Florence. The journey by car into Pisa takes around 5 minutes; Florence is just over an hour away by road. The smaller Aeroporto di Firenze (tel: 055 306 1300; www.aeroporto-firenze.it) is 6.5km (4 miles) from Pisa.

BY RAIL AND ROAD

Travellers from Britain can take the Eurostar service to Paris or Brussels, then direct trains to Rome, Florence, Milan, Turin and Venice. Most of the Rome services take you to Stazione Termini, but some long-distance services go to Ostiense or Tiburtina, both on the edge of the city. The journey time from London (St Pancras) to Italy is between 11 and 15 hours, depending on your destination; sleepers are available from Paris.

Every land route into Italy from the rest of Europe crosses the Alps via one of the passes or tunnels (St Gotthard, Great St Bernard, Frejus and Mont Blanc). From the Channel routes head south through France, Switzerland and Germany. There are toll roads along the way, and the journey to the Italian border from northern France takes 11–14 hours.

BY SEA

Ferries from Greece land at Ancona, Bari and Venice. Travellers heading for Sicily will find regular ferry crossings from Naples, Reggio di Calabria and Genoa; for Sardinia, there are ferries from Genoa, Livorno and Civitavecchia.

Getting around

PUBLIC TRANSPORT

Internal flights Services throughout the country are provided by Alitalia (tel: 06 65 643; www.alitalia.com). A more limited list of destinations is offered by Meridiana (tel: 892 928) and Air One (tel: 06 4888 0069).

Trains Italian State Railways (Ferrovie dello Stato, or FS; www.fs-on-line.com) has an efficient range of services. Regionale, Diretto and Espresso trains stop at every station; Intercity trains cost more but are faster; and the Pendolino is the fastest and most expensive.

Long-distance buses There is no national bus company but Eurolines (☎ 055 357 110; www.eurolines.com) offers a service between the main Italian towns and several cities outside Italy. Each major city has its own companies for short-, medium- and some long-distance coach travel.

Ferries Genoa and Naples are the main ports for the Mediterranean, with regular services to Sicily and Sardinia (www.traghettionline.it). Naples also has services to Capri and other islands, including fast hydrofoils during the height of the summer season. On the Adriatic, Brindisi and Otranto are well served by ferries to Greece. Book well in advance for car ferries. The Italian Lakes, in the north of the country, also have ferries between the towns around their shores. Venice has a comprehensive network of water transport, including *vaporetti* and the faster *motoscafi*, following fixed routes along the canals and the lagoon.

Urban transport Buses are the best way to get around towns of any size. Bus stops *(fermate)* are clearly marked with the routes. You need a ticket before boarding at the rear *(entrata),* where you stamp it in the machine. Exit through the middle door *(uscita)*. Some cities have trams, which run like buses. Venice has water buses *(vaporetti)*, and Milan and Rome have underground trains. Tickets for urban public transport can be bought in tobacconists and newsstands.

TAXIS

Taxis can be hailed in the street, found at taxi stands or reserved by telephone. There's an initial charge and a rate per kilometre. Heavy traffic can mean stiff meter increases and there are Sunday and late-night supplements. In Venice, water taxis are white and have a cabin.

FARES AND TICKETS

Train and internal airline tickets can be bought online, at stations and airports and from some travel agents. In cities, bus and tram tickets must be bought before boarding; they are available at *tabacchi* and newsagents. Tickets must be validated by stamping them in a special machine before travel commences; you'll find these on station platforms and inside public transport vehicles. There are few travel concessions for foreign visitors.

Museums and galleries normally offer some reductions on the entry price for holders of an International Student Identity Card (ISIC) and for EU citizens over the age of 65 on production of an identity card (or passport).

DRIVING

- Drive on the right.
- Speed limit on motorways *(autostrade)*, which have tolls 130kph (80mph); on main roads 110kph (68mph); on secondary roads 90kph (56mph); on urban roads 50kph (31mph).
- Seat belts must be worn in front seats at all times and in rear seats where available.
- Random breath-testing takes place. Never drive under the influence of alcohol.
- Petrol *(benzina)* is expensive. All garages sell unleaded *(senza piombo)* – 95 and 98 octane, diesel *(gasolio)* and liquified petroleum gas (LPG). Outside urban areas filling stations open 7–12:30 and 3–7:30. Motorway services open 24 hours. Credit cards aren't widely accepted away from urban areas. Many automatic pumps take banknotes in denominations of €5, €10 and €20, but may reject older ones.
- In the event of a breakdown, tel: 116, giving your registration number and type of car, and the nearest ACI (Automobile Club d'Italia) office will assist you. This service is free to foreign-registered vehicles or cars rented from Rome or Milan airports (you will need your passport).

CAR RENTAL

Car rental is available at airports, main railway stations and town-centre offices. Small local firms offer the best rates, but cars can only be rented locally. Air and train travellers can book inclusive deals. You need to be over 21 (some companies have a minimum age of 25) and have held a full licence for a year.

Being there

TOURIST OFFICES

Florence ✉ Via Cavour 1 ☎ 055 290 832; www.firenzeturismo.it

Genoa ✉ Stazione Principe ☎ 01 246 2633; www.turismoinliguria.it

Milan ✉ Palazzo del Turismo, Via Marconi 1 ☎ 02 7252 4301; www.milanoinfo.eu

Naples ✉ Via San Carlo 9 ☎ 081 252 5711; www.naples.net

Palermo ✉ Piazza Castelnuovo 34/35 ☎ 091 605 8351; www.palermotourism.it

Rome ✉ Via Parigi 11 ☎ 06 488 991; www.romaturismo.it
There are information kiosks near many of the main tourist sights.

Turin ✉ Stazione di Ferroviaria di Porta Nova ☎ 011 535 901, 011 535 181; www.turismotorino.org

Venice ✉ Piazza San Marco 71/F ☎ 041 529 8711; www.turismovenezia.it

MONEY

The euro (€) is the official currency of Italy, which is divided into 100 cents. Coins come in denominations of 1, 2, 5, 10, 20 and 50 cents, €1 and €2, and notes come in €5, €10, €20, €50, €100, €200 and €500 denominations (the last two are rarely seen). The notes and one side of the coins are the same throughout the European single currency zone, but each country has a different design on one face of each of the coins. Notes and coins from any of the other countries can be used in Italy.

TIPS/GRATUITIES

Yes ✓   No ✕

Restaurants (if service not included)	✓ 10–15%
Cafés/bars	✓ €1 minimum
Taxis	✓ 15%
Porters	✓ €1
Chambermaids	✓ €2 weekly
Toilets	✓ €1 minimum

POSTAL AND INTERNET SERVICES

Rome's main post office is on Piazza San Silvestro 19 (open Mon–Fri 9–6, Sat 9–2, tel: 0800 160 000; www.poste.it), but it is quicker to buy stamps from a *tabacho*.

Italy has numerous internet offices. All airports and some stations have WiFi areas, and most city hotels (3-star and above) have internet access in bedrooms.

TELEPHONES

Most bars have a telephone, and there are many in public places. Most operate with phonecards *(schede telefoniche)*, which can be bought from tobacconists, shops, bars, post offices, newsstands and other places. Some take coins of 10, 20 or 50 cents, €1 or €2, some take credit cards.

Emergency telephone numbers

Police 113
Carabinieri 112
Fire 115

Any emergency
(including Ambulance) 118
Road Assistance (ACI) 116

International dialling codes

From Italy to:
UK: 00 44
Germany: 00 49

USA/Canada: 00 1
Netherlands: 00 31

EMBASSIES AND CONSULATES

UK ☎ 06 4220 0001;
www.britishembassy.gov.uk
Germany ☎ 06 809 551;
www.ambgermania.it
USA ☎ 06 46 741;
www.usembassy.gov

Netherlands ☎ 06 3228 6001;
www.mfa.nl/rom-nl
Spain ☎ 06 684 0401; www.amba-spagna.com

ELECTRICITY

The power supply is 220 volts (125 volts in some parts). Type of socket: round two- or three-hole sockets taking plugs of two round pins, or sometimes three pins in a vertical line. British visitors should bring an adaptor, US visitors will need a voltage transformer.

HEALTH AND SAFETY

Sun advice In summer, particularly in July and August, it can get oppressively hot and humid in cities. If 'doing the sights', cover up and apply a sunscreen, and drink plenty of fluids.

Drugs A pharmacy *(farmacia)*, designated by a green cross sign, has highly trained staff able to offer medical advice on minor ailments and provide a wide range of prescription and non-prescription medicines and drugs. They take turns staying open through the afternoons and into late evening.

Safe water In some rural areas it is not advisable to drink the tap water (*'acqua non potabile'* means 'the water is unsafe to drink'). However, across most of the rest of the country the water is perfectly safe.

Safety Petty theft is the main problem in busy towns and tourist spots. The *carabinieri*, to whom thefts should be reported, wear black uniforms with red stripes down the outer seams of the trousers. Some precautions:
- Carry shoulder bags and cameras slung across your body.
- Scooter-borne bag-snatchers can be foiled if you keep on the inside of the pavement.
- Do not put anything down on a café or restaurant table.

Carabinieri assistance: ☎ 112 from any call box

OPENING HOURS

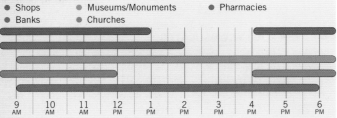

- Shops
- Banks
- Museums/Monuments
- Churches
- Pharmacies

9 AM 10 AM 11 AM 12 PM 1 PM 2 PM 3 PM 4 PM 5 PM 6 PM

Shop opening hours are changing, but generally it is Mon–Sat, with a break from 1 to 4pm. Food shops close on Thu afternoon and others on Mon morning (plus Sat afternoon during summer). Some banks open until 2pm and close in the afternoon. Many museums open in the afternoon (5–7:30pm), others are open all day, and a few open late into the evening. Many museums close around 1pm on Sun, and most are closed Mon.

LANGUAGE

The language you hear on the street will be Italian, even if you are on the Swiss shores of lakes Maggiore and Lugano. There are dialects in the mountains, but even there Italian is the first language. In Italian each syllable is pronounced, so *colazione* would be *col-atz-i-own-ay*. *C* and *g* are always 'hard' (as in cat or gate) before *a*, *o* or *u*, and always 'soft' (as in cello or gin) before *e* or *i*. To get a hard *c* or *g* before an *e* or *i*, Italians insert an *h*, eg Chianti. *Gn* is pronounced *ny*.

yes	*si*	good afternoon	*buongiorno*
no	*non*	goodnight	*buona sera*
please	*per favore*	how are you ?	*come sta ?*
thank you	*grazie*	do you speak	*parla inglese ?*
welcome	*benvenuto*	English?	
goodbye	*arrivederci*	I don't understand	*non capisco*
good morning	*buongiorno*	how much ?	*quanto costa ?*
bank	*banca*	cheque	*cheque*
exchange office	*cambio*	traveller's	*traveller's*
post office	*ufficio postale*	cheque	cheque
coin	*moneta*	credit card	*carta di credito*
banknote	*banconote*	exchange rate	*corse del cambio*
café	*caffè*	beer	*birra*
waiter	*cameriere*	wine	*vino*
waitress	*cameriera*	water	*acqua*
bill	*conto*	coffee	*caffè*
airport	*aeroporto*	boat	*battello*
train	*treno*	ticket	*biglietto*
station	*stazione*	single ticket	*andante*
bus	*autobus*	return ticket	*andante e ritorno*
bus stop	*fermata d'autobus*	car	*machina*
hotel	*albergo*	reservation	*prenotazione*
single room	*singola*	room service	*servizio nella stanza*
double room	*matrimoniale*	toilet	*gabinetto*

Best places to see

1 Basilica di San Pietro and Il Vaticano, Rome

www.vatican.va/museums

One of the world's biggest churches half fills one of its smallest states – the Vatican, headquarters of the Roman Catholic church and home to a vast museum.

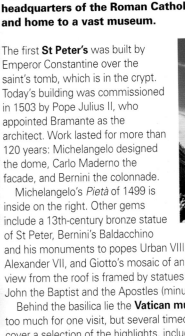

The first **St Peter's** was built by Emperor Constantine over the saint's tomb, which is in the crypt. Today's building was commissioned in 1503 by Pope Julius II, who appointed Bramante as the architect. Work lasted for more than 120 years: Michelangelo designed the dome, Carlo Maderno the facade, and Bernini the colonnade.

Michelangelo's *Pietà* of 1499 is inside on the right. Other gems include a 13th-century bronze statue of St Peter, Bernini's Baldacchino and his monuments to popes Urban VIII and Alexander VII, and Giotto's mosaic of an angel. The view from the roof is framed by statues of Christ, John the Baptist and the Apostles (minus St Peter).

Behind the basilica lie the **Vatican museums** – too much for one visit, but several timed routes cover a selection of the highlights, including the Museo Gregoriano-Egizio Egyptian collection; the Museo Chiaramonti collection of Roman sculpture; the Museo Pio Clementino, whose ancient art includes the Belvedere Apollo and Laocoön; the

Museo Gregoriano–Etrusco's Greek, Roman and Etruscan art; and corridors of tapestries and 16th-century maps that lead to the four Raphael rooms. In the first is the famous School of Athens in which many of Raphael's contemporaries are portrayed as Greek philosophers and poets. The other rooms show biblical and early Christian scenes.

Next comes the Sistine Chapel. Michelangelo painted the ceiling between 1508 and 1512. The ceiling tells the story of the Creation, in which God is dividing light from darkness and water from land before creating the sun, the moon, Adam and Eve. The last four panels show the birth of original sin and the story of Noah. On the chapel's end wall is Michelangelo's much later *Last Judgement.*

Beyond the chapel are the Vatican library, a gallery of modern religious art, and collections of pagan and early Christian antiquities. The Pinacoteca (picture gallery) has a marvellous collection of medieval, Renaissance and baroque paintings, with masterpieces by most of the famous names in European art.

✠ *Roma 1c* 🚇 Ottaviano 🚌 To Piazza del Risorgimento
ℹ Vatican Tourist Office ☎ 06 6988 4466
Basilica di San Pietro
🕐 Apr–Sep daily 7–7; Oct–Mar daily 7–6 ✋ Basilica: free; roof: moderate
Musei Vaticani
🕐 7 Mar–29 Oct, 27 Dec–6 Jan Mon–Sat 10–4:45; 7 Jan–6 Mar, 2 Nov–24 Dec Mon–Sat 10–1:45; last Sun each month 9–1:45. Closed 1, 6 Jan, 11 Feb, 19 Mar, Easter Mon, 1, 20 May, 10, 29 Jun, 15, 16 Aug, 8, 25, 26 Dec ✋ Expensive
🍴 Cafeteria (€)

2 Canal Grande, Venice

Dissecting the city, the Canal Grande is Venice's main thoroughfare, a magnificent, sinuous waterway lined with a procession of glorious buildings and *palazzi* that is unique in the world.

Running northwest to southeast, the Canal Grande is almost 4km (2.5 miles) long and varies in width from 30–70m (100–230ft), with an average depth of around 5m (16ft). Three *sestiere* (city wards), Cannaregio, San Marco and Castello, lie to the east

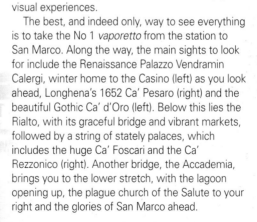

and three, San Polo, Santa Croce and Dorsoduro, to the west. The Canal is spanned by four bridges and served by seven *traghetti* stations, from which gondolas ply back and forth across its width. Lining its banks is an uninterrupted sequence of *palazzi* and churches, their main facades overlooking the water. Built over a period of more than four centuries, these superlative buildings stylistically cover the whole span of Venetian architecture, their combination of water, stone and light one of the world's truly great visual experiences.

The best, and indeed only, way to see everything is to take the No 1 *vaporetto* from the station to San Marco. Along the way, the main sights to look for include the Renaissance Palazzo Vendramin Calergi, winter home to the Casino (left) as you look ahead, Longhena's 1652 Ca' Pesaro (right) and the beautiful Gothic Ca' d'Oro (left). Below this lies the Rialto, with its graceful bridge and vibrant markets, followed by a string of stately palaces, which includes the huge Ca' Foscari and the Ca' Rezzonico (right). Another bridge, the Accademia, brings you to the lower stretch, with the lagoon opening up, the plague church of the Salute to your right and the glories of San Marco ahead.

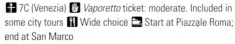

🚻 7C (Venezia) 🖐 *Vaporetto* ticket: moderate. Included in some city tours 🍴 Wide choice 🚤 Start at Piazzale Roma; end at San Marco
ℹ Piazza San Marco, San Marco 71f ☎ 041 529 8711

Costiera Amalfitana

www.amalficoastweb.com
www.amalfitouristoffice.it

South of Naples lies the Amalfi Coast, a stretch of spectacular coastline, where ragged, grey cliffs plunge into an unbelievably turquoise Mediterranean.

Despite being one of Italy's busiest holiday haunts, it is still possible, among the summer crowds that fill the white fishing-villages-turned resorts, to feel the romance that has inspired generations of artists and songwriters. Even slightly over-developed Sorrento, a centre for package tours on the western end of the Costiera, has its peaceful corners, with views over the Bay of Naples to the islands of Capri (➤ 176) and Ischia. Further east is the more chic and expensive resort of Positano, clinging to the cliffside.

North and a little inland from here is **Ravello,** arguably the most stunning of the Amalfitana towns. The sea views are particularly good from exotic Villa Rufolo. Wagner stayed here in 1880 and based the magic gardens in *Parsifal* on those of the villa. The gardens of the Villa Cimbrone are equally evocative. Ravello's 11th-century Cathedral of San Pantaleone was renovated in the 18th century, but the bronze doors by Barisano da Trani (1179) have survived along with other elements of the earlier building, including an ornate 13th-century pulpit.

Amalfi is the largest town and, until the 12th century, it was a major maritime power. Its most

eye-catching sight is the 9th-century Cathedral of Sant'Andrea – although the sumptuous facade is a 19th-century restoration of a 13th-century original. Alongside is the 13th-century Chiostro del Paradiso (Cloister of Paradise), where Amalfi's most illustrious citizens were laid to rest.

✚ 14L

Ravello

ℹ Piazza Duomo 10 ☎ 089 857 977

Amalfi

ℹ Via delle Repubbliche Marinare 19 ☎ 089 871 107

4 Duomo, Milan

www.duomomilano.it

The massive yet delicate Gothic Milan Cathedral, towering above its own vast, open piazza, is dramatically surrounded by bustling, modern Milan.

Even allowing for the decades it usually took to complete a cathedral, the Duomo of Milan was a long time in the making. Work started in 1386 under Prince Gian Galeazzo Visconti, continued over the following centuries in the hands of a host of European craftsmen, and was finished in 1809 under the orders of Napoleon. A trip up to the roof, with its views over Milan to the Alps glimpsed through a forest of 135 spires and 2,244 statues,

makes the long centuries of toil seem worthwhile.

At 157m (515ft) long and 92m (301ft) wide, this is the third-largest church in Europe after St Peter's (► 36–37) and Seville Cathedral. The facade is a surprisingly harmonious mishmash of styles from largely Gothic, through Renaissance and baroque to neoclassical. Beyond the bas-relief bronze doors depicting scenes from the lives of the Virgin and St Ambrose (Milan's patron saint), as well as Milanese history, is a contrastingly bare interior with 52 columns, each 48m (157ft) high, and numerous tombs and memorials lit by glorious 15th- and 16th-century stained-glass windows. Look in particular for a 12th-century bronze candelabrum and the gruesome statue of the flayed St Bartholomew holding his skin. The repeated symbol of a snake swallowing a man was the local Visconti family crest. The crypt contains the usual church treasures, as well as traces of the original 4th-century baptistery.

In the Museo del Duomo (Cathedral Museum), at Piazza del Duomo 14, the history of the cathedral's construction is shown alongside historic artefacts.

✚ 3B (Milano) ☎ 02 8646 3456. Museum: 02 860 358
🕓 Treasury, crypt and roof: mid-Nov to Feb daily 9–4:45; Mar to mid-Nov daily 9–5:45. Baptistery: daily 9:45–12:45, 2:45–5:45. Museum: closed for restoration 🎫 Museum and roof: moderate; treasury and crypt: inexpensive
🍴 Cafeteria (€)

5 Foro Romano, Palatino and Colosseo, Rome

www.capitolium.org
www.romaturismo.it

These atmospheric ruins represent the social, political, religious and business heart of ancient Rome.

You are immersed in Rome's history as soon as you enter the **Forum.** Left of the entrance is the Basilica Aemilia with traces of coins fused into its floor from a fire in the 5th century. Next, along the Sacred Way, is the (rebuilt) 3rd-century Curia where the Senate met, and the rostrum where orations were made. Opposite the Curia are three beautiful columns from the Temple of Castor and Pollux. The round building is the Temple of Vesta – the vestal virgins lived in the villa behind it. Opposite are the three massive vaults of the 4th-century AD Basilica of Maxentius and Constantine. The Arch of Titus, near the exit, was erected in the 1st century AD to celebrate the Emperor's sack of Jerusalem.

On the **Palatine Hill** overlooking the Forum are the remains of the emperors' gigantic palaces and traces of 7th-century BC huts.

The **Colosseum** was built by Emperor Vespasian in the 1st century AD. Tiered seating for more than 55,000 spectators overlooked a central ring where gladiators, other combatants and wild animals (kept in underground passages) fought each other to the death. Mock sea battles could also be staged, thanks to an underground water supply which allowed the arena to be flooded. Changing public

taste and the fall of Rome forced the Colosseum into disuse in the mid-6th century.

Foro Romano and Palatino

✚ *Roma 6e* ✉ Via dei Fori Imperiali ☎ 06 3996 7700 (recorded information) 🕐 Daily 9am to 1 hour before sunset. Closed 1 Jan and 25 Dec ✋ Foro free; Palatino expensive (includes Colosseo)

Colosseo

✚ *Roma 7e* ✉ Piazza del Colosseo ☎ 06 3996 7700 🕐 Daily 9am to 1 hour before sunset ✋ Included in Palatino

6 Galleria degli Uffizi, Florence

www.firenzemusei.it/uffizi

Generations of the powerful Medici family amassed this collection of 13th- to 18th-century paintings, which is among the finest in the world.

The Uffizi, designed by Giorgio Vasari in 1560, was originally intended to house the government offices *(uffici)* of Florence and became home to the Medici art collections in 1588. The art was bequeathed to the city in 1737 by Anna Maria Luisa, the last of the Medici dynasty. Inside, 45 galleries are filled with world-famous masterpieces, hung in roughly chronological order to give an opulent overview of the development of mainly Italian art.

Early highlights include Giotto's *Ognissanti Madonna* (1310), showing his – for its time – revolutionary naturalism and use of perspective. Contrast it with the flatter Gothic styles of Simone Martini, Cimabue and Duccio. Throughout the 15th century the representation of perspective developed as the Renaissance got under way. Look for this in Paolo Uccello's *Battle of San Romano* (1456), Piero della Francesca's imposing profiles of the *Duke and Duchess of Urbino* (1465–70) and Fra Filippo Lippi's *Virgin and Child*. The magnificent Botticelli collection includes the *Birth of Venus* (1485) and *Primavera*

(1478) and there are two Leonardo da Vinci works: an *Annunciation* (1472–75) and an unfinished *Adoration of the Magi* (1481).

Michelangelo's *Holy Family* (1456), with its contorted poses and sculpted, draped fabrics, is an early example of Mannerism. Highlights from this period include Raphael's *Madonna of the Goldfinch* (1506), Parmigianino's *Madonna of the Long Neck* (1534), Titian's sultry *Venus of Urbino* (1538) and works by Caravaggio. Among the non-Italian masters represented are Cranach, Dürer, Holbein, Rubens, Van Dyck, Goya and Rembrandt.

✚ 5E (Firenze) ✉ Loggiata degli Uffizi 6 ☎ 055 238 8651 🕐 Tue–Sun 8:15–6:50 (reservations advised: 055 294 883). Closed Mon, 1 Jan, 1 May, 25 Dec ✋ Expensive 🍴 Cafeteria (€) 🚌 3, 11, 15, 23

7 Piazza San Marco, Venice

Generations of Venetians and visitors have frequented the smart, porticoed cafés that flank this vast, paved square.

The northeast side of the square is dominated by the facade and domes of the **Basilica di San Marco,** built between the 10th and 12th centuries, and added to over 300 years. Above the main entrance are copies of four 3rd-century or older bronze horses, looted from Constantinople in 1204; the originals are inside. The atrium contains superb Romanesque and Byzantine carvings and mosaics and gives access to the interior, covered with glittering mosaics from the 12th to 17th centuries. Treasures, such as the 14th-century Pala d'Oro altar screen, reflect Venice's strong Byzantine links, while the superb tessellated floor highlights the building's age. There are fabulous views from the adjoining 99m-high (325ft) Campanile.

Next to the basilica is the Palazzo Ducale (Doges' Palace), residence of the doges of Venice since the 9th century; the present Gothic building is late 14th century. Inside are the imposing meeting rooms of the

élite groups who ran Venice's complex internal and foreign affairs, lined with wall and ceiling paintings, many by Tintoretto and Veronese. The torture chamber and a labyrinth of dank prison cells hints at the far from benign nature of some aspects of Venetian government. Suspects were brought into the prison via the famous Bridge of Sighs behind the *palazzo*.

The **Museo Correr** is at the opposite end of the piazza. Its collections tell the story of the history of Venice and include sculptures by Canova and a picture gallery; it also stages temporary exhibitions.

✠ 7C (Venezia) 🍴 Plenty of cafés (€€€)

Basilica di San Marco

☎ 041 522 5205 🕓 May–Sep Mon–Sat 9:45–5:30 (4:30 Oct–Apr), Sun 2–4 ✋ Free

Museo Correr

☎ 041 520 9070 🕓 May–Oct daily 9–7; Nov–Apr daily 9–5 ✋ Expensive

8 Pompei

www.pompeiisites.org

The remains of this busy ancient city, buried when Vesuvius erupted in AD79, give some poignant glimpses of daily life in the Roman Empire.

Pompei has been under excavation for more than 250 years and, although only a few buildings are open to the public, there is far too much to see in one day. It is best to buy a detailed guide and map, visit your priority sights, and then wander to absorb the remarkable atmosphere of this beautiful site. Many of the major artistic finds are on display in the Museo Archeologico Nazionale (National Archaeological Museum) in Naples (➤ 172).

Among the most interesting houses are patrician and middle-class villas with statues, mosaics and frescoes, many of them erotic and/or mystic and difficult to interpret. Try to see the Casa dei Vetii,

the Casa del Fauno, the Casa del Poeta Tragico with its 'beware of the dog' sign and, if it's open, the Casa dei Misteri. Shops include a bakery, a cramped brothel with graphic wall paintings of the services offered, and a laundry where you can follow the complicated washing procedures used by ancient Romans. There are also numerous bars and food shops, many with large clay storage pots embedded into their serving hatches.

Public buildings include the forum with its basilica and temples, two

theatres, Italy's oldest surviving amphitheatre (80BC), baths and two gyms.

Throughout Pompei the cobbled streets are heavily grooved by the passage of inumerable carts, and the walls are spattered with snatches of carefully executed graffiti. The most moving memorials of the disaster are the casts of bodies of the victims (believed to be about 10 per cent of the 25,000 population), eternally frozen in the positions in which they died.

➕ 14L ✉ Piazza Esedra 5, Pompei ☎ 081 857 5347
🕐 Apr–Oct daily 8:30–7:30 (last admission 6); Nov–Mar daily 8:30–5 (last admission 3:30). Closed 1 Jan, 25 Dec
✋ Expensive 🍴 Cafeteria (€)

9 Ravenna's Mosaics

www.turismo.ra.it
www.ravennamosaici.it

Ravenna, once capital of the Roman Empire, boasts 5th- to 6th-century churches containing the world's most accomplished Byzantine mosaics.

While much of the rest of western Europe was in Dark Ages decline, Ravenna was enjoying prosperity as an important provincial centre and, from around AD402, as the western capital of the Roman Empire. The city converted to Christianity in the 2nd century and much of its wealth went into building churches and other religious sites. The mosaics contain some of the earliest versions of Christian images such as the baptism of Christ, the Virgin, saints, martyrs and apostles with their symbols, and the cross. The best are housed in the following five sites across the historic centre.

The 5th-century **Battistero (Baptistery) Neoniano** is believed to be Ravenna's oldest monument. The mosaics show the baptism of Christ and the 12 Apostles. The cruciform

Mausoleo (Mausoleum) di Galla Placidia (started in AD430) may not contain the remains of Galla, sister of Emperor Honorius, but it does have charming mosaics of stars and flowers on the vaults and a Good Shepherd on the west wall. The dome

of the **Battistero degli Ariani** (late 5th century) shows another baptism of Christ.

The finest mosaics in Ravenna are in two churches. **Sant'Apollinare Nuovo** (AD519) contains processions of saints bearing gifts to the Virgin and scenes from the life of Christ, all with gold backgrounds. **San Vitale** (consecrated AD547) has richly coloured mosaics full of flowers and birds and depicting Christ the King, Old Testament scenes, and Empress Theodora and Emperor Justinian.

✚ 6D ☎ 0544 541 688 (for advance booking) 🕐 Apr–Sep daily 9–7; Mar, Oct daily 9:30–5:30; Nov–Feb daily 10–5 (except Battistero degli Ariani; see below) ✋ A combined entrance ticket (€€€) to the main locations offers considerable savings. In high season book online at www.ravennamosaici.it. Tour starts at Sant'Apollinare Nuovo

Battistero Neoniano
✉ Via Battistero 🕐 See above ✋ Expensive
Mausoleo di Galla Placidia
✉ Via Fiandrini 🕐 See above ✋ Expensive
Battistero degli Ariani
✉ Vicolo degli Ariani ☎ 0544 543 711 🕐 Daily 8:30–4:30 ✋ Free
Sant'Apollinare Nuovo
✉ Via di Roma 🕐 See above ✋ Expensive
San Vitale
✉ Via Fiandrini 🕐 See above ✋ Expensive

10 Valle dei Templi, Sicily

www.parcovalledeitempli.it

The most extensive ancient Greek remains outside Greece, these nine ruined temples were once part of the city of Akragas.

Akragas (now Agrigento) was founded in 582BC by settlers from Rhodes. For nearly 200 years it flourished, with a temple complex that rivalled that of Athens. In 406BC, it was attacked by the Carthaginians, who pillaged the temples. Destruction was continued by zealous 6th-century Christians and earthquakes.

Eight of the temples lie west to east along a ridge south of Agrigento. Little remains of the Tempio di Vulcano (430BC), but nearby is a group of shrines for sacrifices to the underground (chthonic) gods. The strikingly positioned three columns are part of the so-called Tempio dei Dioscuri (Castor and Pollux), a 19th-century assemblage of bits and pieces from several buildings. Further on is the unfinished Tempio di Giove (Olympian Zeus), started in 480BC. Eight erect columns belong to the Tempio di Ercole (Hercules), built in 520BC and probably the oldest survivor in the valley. The Tempio della Concordia (Concord, 430BC) is well preserved. The 450BC Tempio di Hera (Juno) is set dramatically on top of the ridge. South is the Tempio di Esculapio (Aesculepius, god of healing).

➕ *Sicilia 2e* (Agrigento) ✉ Valle dei Templi, Agrigento; Via Sacra, Agrigento ☎ 0922 621 611 🕐 Apr–Sep daily 9–6; Oct–Mar daily 9–4 ✋ Expensive 🍴 Restaurant and bar at entrance on site (€€) 🚌 Bus from Agrigento

Best things to do

Good places to have lunch

Antico Giardinetto (€€)
This long-established restaurant, with its pretty garden for summer dining, specializes in classic Venetian fish dishes.
✉ Santa Croce 2253, Calle dei Morti, Venice ☎ 041 722 882

Cecilia Metella (€€)
Evocative shady garden with fountains and statues.
✉ Via Appia Antica 125–129, Rome ☎ 06 511 0213

Certosa di Maggiano (€€€)
Tuscan cuisine in a delightful setting in an old monastery.
✉ Via Certosa 82, Siena ☎ 0577 288 180

Don Alfonso (€€€)
One of the best restaurants in the south, with an excellent *menù degustazione* (tasting menu).
✉ Corso Sant'Agata 11–13, Sant'Agata Sui Due Golfi, Naples
☎ 081 533 0508

Frantoio (€€€)
Best of Ligurian sea specialities in the heart of this pretty old town south of the Cinque Terre.
✉ Via Cavour 21, Lerici, La Spezia ☎ 0187 964 174

Grappolo Blu (€–€€)
A charming, low-key restaurant that specializes in the best Tuscan food, along with the great wines of Montalcino.
✉ Via Scale di Moglio 1, Montalcino ☎ 0577 847150

Osteria del Binari (€€)
This lovely rustic restaurant, with its cool garden, makes an ideal place to enjoy fixed-price, traditional meals, elegantly presented.
✉ Via Tortona 1, Milan ☎ 02 8940 9428

Sandro al Navile (€€€)

Good example of the cuisine of one of Italy's gastronomic capitals.

✉ Via del Sostegno 15, Bologna ☎ 051 634 3100

Sora Margherita (€)

Great home cooking in a traditional *trattoria* in the Roman Ghetto.

✉ Piazza delle Cinque Scole 30, Rome ☎ 06 687 4216

Stella (€€)

Immensely popular restaurant for al fresco dining, serving good traditional Sicilian cooking and a full range of *pizze*.

✉ Via Alloro 104, Palermo, Sicily ☎ 091 606 1136

Beautiful *piazzas*

Campo dei Miracoli, Pisa

Pisa's most famous landmark, the 54m (177ft) Leaning Tower
(Torre Pendente; ➤ 137), is one of four dreamlike monuments on
the harmoniously perfect Campo dei Miracoli (Piazza del Duomo).

Il Campo, Siena

This is a dramatic, sloping, shell-shaped *piazza*, with the 13th- to
14th-century Palazzo Pubblico (➤ 140–141) at its foot, topped by
the 102m (334ft) Torre del Mangia, which offers excellent views.

Piazza Brà, Verona

The biggest square in Verona (➤ 114) has the largest Roman

amphitheatre in the world, which is still in use today as a summer venue for performances of opera.

Piazza del Duomo, Milan
For a piece of Gothic in downtown Milan (► 42–43).

Piazza Navona, Rome
This is one of the world's most beautiful squares (► 155); its focus is Bernini's spectacular Fontana dei Fiumi (1651), in front of the church of Sant'Agnese in Agone.

Piazza del Popolo, Ascoli Piceno
For its elegant Renaissance portico (► 132).

Piazza San Marco, Venice
Smart cafés flank the most famous square in the world (► 48–49), its northeast side dominated by the ornate facade of Basilica di San Marco, with the Palazzo Ducale (Doges' Palace) next door and the Museo Correr at the opposite end.

Piazza dei Signori, Verona
The heart of medieval Verona (► 114).

Piazza dei Signori, Vicenza
World-renowned classical architect Andrea Palladio's first public commission – here in his home town – was the graceful double-colonnaded Basilica in Piazza dei Signori (► 115).

Piazza della Signoria, Florence
The political and social heart of Florence, this is an outdoor art gallery with Ammanati's Fontana di Nettuno (1575) and a copy of Michelangelo's *David* among the works that stand outside the Loggia dei Lanzi (1382), itself containing fine Roman statues (► 126).

Stunning views

Great beaches

Costiera Amalfitana
Dramatic seaside towns and villages (► 40–41).

Costiera Calabrese (Calabrian Coast)
For relatively undeveloped beaches and bays between cliffs
(► 177).

Gargano
For white sand coves and turquoise water, backed by dense pines
(► 178).

Riviera Ligure (Ligurian Coast)
For fishing villages with a veneer of sophistication (► 90–91).

Sardinia
For beaches that run the gamut from the jet-set resorts of the
Costa Smeralda to deserted stretches of sand, some only
accessible by boat (► 180–181).

Best frescoes

Cappella degli Scrovegni, Padua, by Giotto (▶ 110–111)

Cappella Sistina, Rome, by Michelangelo (▶ 37)

San Francesco, Arezzo, by Piero della Francesca (▶ 131)

Santa Maria del Carmine, Florence, by Masaccio (▶ 128)

Santa Maria delle Grazie, Milan, by Leonardo da Vinci (▶ 83)

a walk

through Dorsoduro, Venice

After visiting Santa Maria della Salute, designed by Baldassare Longhena and built between 1631 and 1681 in thanksgiving at the end a plague outbreak, cross the bridge and follow the yellow wall signs to the Accademia.

Along the way, you'll pass the Collezione Peggy Guggenheim, a fabulous museum of 20th-century art housed in an unfinished 18th-century *palazzo*. Campo San Vio is a good place to sit beside the Grand Canal and watch the water traffic.

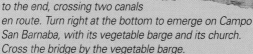

Continue past the Accademia bridge and the museum and follow the route to the next canal. Turn left here and walk all the way down beside the canal, looking for the gondola workshop, the squero, *on the opposite bank. At the bottom, the wide Canale della Giudecca opens out; turn right, cross the bridge and walk along the Zattere waterfront, taking the first right, very narrow Calle Trevisan. Follow this all the way to the end, crossing two canals en route. Turn right at the bottom to emerge on Campo San Barnaba, with its vegetable barge and its church. Cross the bridge by the vegetable barge.*

This is the Ponte dei Pugni, the scene of violent, but sanctioned, brawls in medieval times; note the footprints on the top steps which mark the starting point for the fights.

Now continue up the broad Rio Tera Canal, swinging left at the top to reach the wide-open expanse of Campo Santa Margherita, one of Venice's liveliest squares and the focal point for the sestiere *of Dorsoduro.*

Distance 3.5km (2 miles)
Time 1.5 hours, or 5 hours if visiting the Guggenheim and Accademia
Start point San Maria della Salute *vaporetto* stop
End point Campo Santa Margherita
Lunch L'Incontro (€) ✉ Dorsoduro 3062a, Campo Santa Margherita
☎ 041 522 2404 🚫 Closed Mon

BEST THINGS TO DO

Places to take the children

Acquario di Genova
Europe's biggest aquarium, with dolphins among the attractions.
✉ Piazza Caricamento, Genova ☎ 010 234 5666; www.acquario.ge.it

Acquasplash
Acquasplash has something for all ages; four swimming pools and some spectacular flumes and slides, including the Black Hole.
✉ Via Dalle Chiesa 3, Corte Franca, Brescia ☎ 030 982 6441;
www.acquasplash.it

Biopark
Rome's renamed and much improved zoo has a good range of animals and play areas for children of all ages.
✉ Piazzale del Giardino Zoologico 1 ☎ 06 360 8211; www.villaborghese.it

Città dei Bambini
A state-of-the-art, hands-on science and technology museum, where play is used to teach 3- to 14-year-olds about the scientific and natural worlds. Attractions include everything from a working TV studio to a giant anthill.
✉ Magazzini del Cotone, Genova ☎ 010 247 5702; www.cittadeibambini.net

Città della Domenica
As well as a zoo and reptile house, 'Sunday City' has a few imaginative rides and themed attractions, including Tarzan's house, Sleeping Beauty's castle and a maze.
✉ Località Monte Pulito, Perugia ☎ 075 505 4941;
www.cittadelladomenica.com

Edenlandia
A theme park packed with a massive range of rides and attractions based on, among other themes, the Wild West, historic China, life in a castle and sci-fi.
✉ Viale Kennedy, Napoli ☎ 081 239 9693; www.edenlandia.it

Fiabilandia

Theme park, with rides to the lake of dreams and into a mine in the Grand Canyon. There is also a puppet and model museum and a vast swimming pool. New attractions are added annually.

✉ Via Cardano, Rivazzurra, Rimini ☎ 0541 372 064; www.fiabilandia.it

Gardaland

Italy's biggest and best theme park has six theme villages, including vertiginous rides, a pirates' galleon, a treasure hunt with Indiana Jones in ancient Egypt and a journey through time.

✉ Località Ronchi, Castelnuovo del Garda ☎ 045 644 9777; www.gardaland.it

Luna Park

This funfair may be showing its age, but it still provides good, old-fashioned family fun.

✉ Via delle Tre Fontane, Roma ☎ 06 592 5933; www.luneur.it

Mirabilandia

A massive theme park divided into eight distinct areas catering for all ages. *L'Evolution* is the biggest transportable big wheel in the world (35m/115ft high).

✉ SS Adriatica Km 162, Savio (between Rimini and Ravenna) ☎ 0544 561 111; www.mirabilandia.it

Best cities for shopping

Florence (Firenze)

The range of shopping here includes leather goods, crafts, paper products, jewellery and high fashion. The principal shopping area is north of the river, on Via Tornabuoni, Via dei Calzauoli and around the Piazza della Repubblica.

Milan (Milano)

Milan is home to most of the big names in fashion design, and there's a growing street-fashion scene, too. There are also good commercial art galleries. Head for the Quadrilatero d'Oro (Golden Rectangle) around Via Monte Napoleone.

Rome (Roma)

The Italian capital is packed with clothes and shoe shops, fashion houses and places specializing in crafts and artisan foods. Explore the areas around Piazza di Spagna and Via dei Condotti.

Turin (Torino)

Cutting-edge designer fashions and trendy unique items are the

draw here, and there's a good range of chain-stores and food shops – notably those selling chocolates.

Venice (Venezia)

World-famous for its glass, Venice also has a great range of textiles and marbled paper. Carnival masks, unique to this city, are also available from workshops where they are made. The streets around Vallaresso are good for fashion houses, or explore on either side of the Rialto Bridge.

Good souvenirs

Ceramics and pottery
Every region of Italy produces wonderful artisan ceramics and pottery, often created from centuries-old designs. Deruta (Umbria), Naples (Tuscany) and Sciacca (Sicily) have some of the best.

Designer fashion and shoes
Milan is the heartland of Italian fashion design, but Rome has fashion houses, too, and all the big names are represented in most of the bigger cities in Italy.

Glassware
Venetian coloured glass made on the island of Murano is superb, and there are several outlets within the city.

Olive oil and wine
Featuring so strongly in Italian cuisine, it's hardly surprising that top-quality olive oil is widely available. Tuscany is a good place to buy both oil and wine; northeast Italy also has good wines.

Religious memorabilia
Rome's Vatican City is awash with religious souvenirs for its many visitors and pilgrims; Naples specializes in nativity scenes.

Best museums

Ca' Rezzonico, Venice

This sumptuous *palazzo* on the Grand Canal houses a museum of 17th-century life, Venice's most hedonistic era. You'll find magnificent furniture, textiles, glass and great paintings in opulently decorated rooms overlooking the water, and a tranquil courtyard garden.

Galleria dell'Accademia, Venice
(► 100–101)

Galleria Borghese, Rome
(► 153)

Galleria degli Uffizi, Florence
(► 46–47)

Museo Archeologico Nazionale, Naples
(► 172)

Museo Nazionale del Bargello, Florence
(► 124)

Musei Vaticani, Rome
(► 36–37)

Palazzo Doria Pamphilj, Rome
(► 154)

Palazzo Pitti, Florence
(► 125)

Pinacoteca Ambrosiana, Milan
(► 82)

Places to stay

ALBEROBELLO
Dei Trulli (€€€)

Live in your own *trullo* (➤ 174), furnished in Mediterranean style, in a pretty park with restaurant, swimming pool and children's playground.

✉ Via Cadore 32 ☎ 080 432 3555; www.hoteldeitrulli.it

FLORENCE
Loggiato dei Serviti (€€€)

Set on one of Florence's loveliest *piazze*, this rambling old hotel, in a former monastery a few steps from the Duomo, has beautifully furnished rooms with beamed ceilings and every comfort.

✉ Piazza Santissima Annunziata 3 ☎ 055 289 592;
www.loggiatodeiservitihotel.it

GENOA
Hotel Bristol Palace (€€€)

Top-class old hotel (although the grandeur is fading a little) with 133 rooms, in a fashionable part of the city.

✉ Via XX Settembre 35 ☎ 010 592 541; www.hotelbristolpalace.it

LAGO DI COMO
Grand Hotel Villa Serbelloni (€€€)

This beautiful hotel, in a villa beside the lakeshore, oozes with old-style luxurious living, but with modern services.

✉ Via Roma 1, Bellagio ☎ 031 950 216; www.villaserbelloni.com
🕐 Closed Nov–Mar

NAPLES
Vesuvio (€€€)

An elegant, luxury hotel with views over Porta Santa Lucia. It has stylish décor and antique furnishings, two restaurants, a sports club, sauna and limousine service.

✉ Via Partenope 45 ☎ 081 764 0044; www.vesuvio.it

ROME
Albergo Cesari (€€)

This comfortable hotel in an 18th-century *palazzo* has traditionally furnished rooms and a roof terrace, and is close to the Pantheon.

✉ Via di Pietra 89a ☎ 06 674 9701; www.albergocesari.it

Campo dei Fiori (€€)

In one of the loveliest quarters of the capital's centre, this hotel (terrace overlooks Roman rooftops) is in a flaking ochre-coloured street. Pleasant décor and multilingual staff.

✉ Via dei Biscione 6 ☎ 06 6880 6865; www.hotelcampodeifiori.com

SAN GIMIGNANO
Antico Pozzo (€€€)

Frescoed or beamed ceilings, antique Tuscan furniture and cool tiled floors are the keynotes of this wonderful hotel.

✉ Via San Matteo 87 ☎ 0577 942 014; www.anticopozzo.com

VENICE
Gritti Palace (€€€)

A dream hotel in a 15th-century *palazzo* on the Grand Canal; one of the best, most luxurious and most expensive in Venice. Private boat to the airport and free transport to a private beach on the Lido.

✉ Campo Santa Maria del Giglio 2467, San Marco ☎ 041 794 611; www.luxurycollection.com/grittipalace

Exploring

Italy was one of the first tourist destinations in the world, with aristocratic Britons heading there in droves during their Grand Tour of Europe.

The attraction has endured and grown to mammoth proportions, and there are many reasons to explore Italy: a wealth of ancient ruins and monuments, spectacular mountain scenery (and winter sports), the gorgeous Italian Lakes in the north, vibrant cities, shops full of chic fashions in Milan and Rome, some of the best museums and art galleries in the world, picturesque coastal villages and beaches, little hilltop towns in Tuscany, boat rides to romantic islands… The list goes on and on.

And then, of course, there's Italian cuisine and world-class wines, and a people who combine a passionate approach to living with a laid back attitude in their day-to-day lives. It's a compelling blend.

Northwest Italy

Here tiny, remote mountain villages clinging to the foothills of the Alps seem to belong to a different world from the sophisticated cities of Milan and Turin, the fashionable resorts of the Riviera and the Lakes, and the historic splendour of medieval and Renaissance towns such as Mantua and Cremona.

Milano

The majestic mountains, the seemingly endless plains and the picture-postcard coasts of northwest Italy provide winter and summer sports that include skiing, mountaineering, swimming and sailing, and vast areas of unspoiled natural charm.

Then there are fantastic art collections and historic monuments, excellent cuisine, and superb *alta moda* shopping. In spite of all this natural and historic beauty, the northwest is also where many of Italy's most important industries and businesses are based, making it among the richest and most productive areas of Europe.

EXPLORING

MILANO (MILAN)

What Rome, Florence and Venice are to romantic,
historic Italy, Milan is to stylish, modern Italy. This busy
metropolis is Italy's second largest city and, while Rome
is the political capital, Milan can claim to be the capital of
business, finance and industry. For most visitors Milan
means chic Italian fashion, stylish bars and restaurants,
bustling streets filled with smartly dressed locals
brandishing *telefonini*, and the chance of seeing opera in
the world-famous Teatro alla Scala (➤ 97). However,
there is even more to Milan, and the city also boasts
some splendid art collections and monuments.

✚ 3B

ℹ️ IAT Piazza Duomo 19a and Piazza Duca d'Aosta 1 ☎ 02 7252
4301; www.milanoinfo.eu

Castello Sforzesco

Most of the castle dates from the 15th century, with
some later additions. It was the seat of the Sforza family,

the dukes of Milan, until the late 19th century when it first housed the city's collections of art, applied arts, archaeology and coins. Among the highlights are Michelangelo's unfinished sculpture, the *Pietà Rondanini*, and pictures by Mantegna, Bellini and Tiepolo; the Museo degli Strumenti Musicali (Musical Instruments Museum); and a collection of 18th- and 19th-century costumes.

www.milanocastello.it

✉ Piazza Castello ☎ 02 8846 3700
🕐 Castle: May–Oct daily 7–7; Nov–Apr daily 7–6. Museum: Tue–Sun 9–5:30. Closed public hols ✋ Castle free; Museum moderate 🚇 Lanza, Cadorna, Cairoli

Duomo

Best places to see, ➤ 42–43.

Galleria d'arte Moderna

This gallery of modern art was opened in 1984 in the Villa Reale and is expanding. The emphasis is on 19th-century Italian artists. Foreign artists are also well represented.

✉ Villa Reale, Via Palestro 16 ☎ 02 8646 3054 🕐 Tue–Sun 9:30–5:30. Closed public hols ✋ Free 🚇 Palestro

Galleria Vittorio Emanuele II

This luxurious 19th-century shopping arcade is packed with
sophisticated shops, bars and restaurants. Look for the zodiac floor
mosaics and representations of Europe, America, Africa and Asia
under the impressive, airy glass dome.

✉ Piazza del Duomo and Piazza della Scala 🚇 Duomo

Pinacoteca Ambrosiana

The *palazzo* was built in 1609 to house Cardinal Federico
Borromeo's art collection and 30,000-volume library. An
immaculate restoration job (1990–97), costing 45 billion *lire*
(well over €21.7 million), has returned it to its original splendour.
The paintings from the 14th to 19th centuries include works by
Caravaggio, Raphael, Tiepolo, Titian and Giorgone. Special
exhibitions occasionally feature some of the library's major
manuscripts, which include a 5th-century illustrated *Iliad*, an early
edition of Dante's *Commedia Divina* and Leonardo's *Atlantic
Codex*.

www.ambrosiana.it

✉ Piazza Pio XI 2 ☎ 02 806 921 🕐 Tue–Sun 10–5:30. Closed public hols
✋ Expensive 🚇 Cordusio

Pinacoteca di Brera

Milan's most important art gallery is housed in a 17th-century *palazzo* which became the Accademia di Belle Arti in the 18th century. Unlike many other Italian collections, this one includes later artists, among them Modigliani, Morandi, Picasso and Braque, as well as the 19th-century Italians, Francesco Hayez and Giovanni Fattori. But earlier periods are particularly well represented too, with masterpieces by Bramante, Caravaggio, Raphael, Canaletto, Van Dyck and Rubens; notable is Mantegna's *Dead Christ*, with its unusual perspective.

✉ Via Brera 28 ☎ 02 722 631; 02 8942 1146 (advance booking)
🕐 Tue–Sun 8:30–7:15 ✋ Moderate 🚇 Lanza, Montenapoleone

Santa Maria delle Grazie

Bramante contributed to this attractive late 15th-century monastery by designing the dome, gallery and cloisters. The gem, however, is in the nearby refectory, where Leonardo da Vinci frescoed his much reproduced *Cenacolo (Last Supper)* on the north wall, between 1485 and 1497. Being a perfectionist, he never quite finished it; but more tragically, over the centuries the ravages of time, damp and warfare have taken their toll and the painting has deteriorated badly. It is nevertheless still spectacular.

✉ Piazza Santa Maria delle Grazie 2, Corso Magenta ☎ 02 8942 1146 🕐 Tue–Sun 8–7:30 (prebooking online or by phone required ✋ Expensive 🚇 Cadorna 🚋 Tram 24 to Corso Magenta

More to see in Northwest Italy

AOSTA
The 'Rome of the Alps' is surrounded by stupendous mountains at the crossroads between the Mont Blanc and St Bernard tunnels. Although mainly used as a holidaymakers' stopover on the way to the Alps, it has an interesting centre with ancient Roman remains. These date back to the 1st century BC, when the city was founded as *Augusta Praetoria*, and include a theatre, an amphitheatre, a forum and the Arco di Augusto.

www.regione.vda.it/turismo

⊞ 1B

🛈 Piazza Chanoux 2 ☎ 0165 33352

CINQUE TERRE
One of the wildest stretches of the Ligurian coastline gets its name from five picturesque villages that cling to cliff edges and tumble down steep hillsides to pretty little bays. Although all the villages can be reached by train, only two of them are easily accessible by road – **Monterosso al Mare,** which is the largest of the Cinque Terre and has the biggest, busiest beaches, and Riomaggiore. Between lie Vernazza, founded by the Romans in a sheltered cove, and Corniglia and Manarola which have wonderful views of the sea. All are linked by steep footpaths.

www.cinqueterre.it

⊞ 4D

Monterosso al Mare

🛈 Piazza Garibaldi 29 ☎ 0187 817 506

CREMONA

Cremona has a strong musical tradition. As well as being the birthplace of composer Claudio Monteverdi (1567–1643), it was where the first violins were made, in the 16th century, and where Antonio Stradivari (1644–1737), or 'Stradivarius' – the most famous violin-maker of all time – had his workshop. His drawings, models and violins can be seen in the **Museo Stradivariano.** The Romanesque-Gothic Duomo (1107–1332) is flanked by the 112m (367ft) Torrazzo tower, with its 15th-century astronomical clock.

www.aptcremona.it; **www.**turismo.comune.cremona.it

✚ 4C

Museo Stradivariano

✉ Via Palestro 17 ☎ 0372 461 886 🕒 Tue–Sat 9–6, Sun and public hols 10–6. Closed 1 Jan, 1 May and 25 Dec ✋ Expensive

ℹ Piazza del Comune 5 ☎ 0372 23233

GENOVA (GENOA)

The birthplace of Christopher Columbus, Genoa has been an important maritime centre since the 11th century, and today its bustling, modern harbours form Italy's most important commercial port. The square 117m-high (383ft) lighthouse, called the *Lanterna* (renovated 1547), used to burn wood to guide ships into port, and the modern aquarium houses an exciting collection of marine life (plant and animal) in reconstructed natural habitats. Behind the Porto Vecchio is the **Duomo (San Lorenzo),** a mix of architectural styles from Romanesque to baroque, with a fine collection of relics in its Museo del Tesoro. Among the most interesting palaces in the city, the Palazzi Bianco and Rosso, on the Via Garibaldi, house important art collections, while the Palazzo del Principe gives an insight into how the aristocratic Doria family lived.

www.turismoinliguria.it

🔁 3D

ℹ️ Piazza Matteotti ☎ 010 868 7452

Duomo San Lorenzo

✉️ Piazza San Lorenzo ☎ 010 345 0048; Museo del Tesoro: 010 247 1831

🕑 Museo: Mon–Sat 9–11, 3–5:30 (guided tours only) 💶 Moderate

Aquarium

✉️ Piazza Caricamento ☎ 010 234 5678; www.acquario.ge.it

🕑 Jul–Aug Mon–Fri 9am–11pm, Sat–Sun 8:45am–11pm; Jan–Jun, Sep–Dec Mon–Fri 9:30–7:30, San–Sun 9:30–8:30 💶 Expensive

LAGO MAGGIORE

This long, mountain-encircled lake runs up into Switzerland. Although some stretches of its banks are overdeveloped, other parts offer the most romantic of idealized lakeside scenery. The lake's most breathtaking features are the three Isole Borromee, owned by the Borromeo family. On Isola Bella, the 17th-century Carlo Borromeo III built a luxurious palace with spectacular gardens for his wife Isabella. Isola dei Pescatori has an attractive village on it, while Isola Madre is covered in gardens. On the lake's shores stand the attractive towns of Angera, Baveno, Cannero Riviera and Verbania (its main centre), holiday destinations since Victorian times.

➕ 3B 🚢 Boats on the lake and to the islands from Verbania

Palazzo Borromeo

www.borromeoturismo.it

✉ Isola Bella ☎ 0323 30 556 🕐 Apr–Oct daily 9–5:30 ✋ Expensive

a drive around Lago di Como

This drive is best avoided on weekends in summer when the roads are particularly crowded.

From Lecco (birthplace of the author Alessandro Manzoni, 1785–1873) cross the River Adda and take statale 583 up the western shore of the lake as far as Onno.

Here you leave the lake, following the road to Valbrona, which has wonderful views west to the Grigne mountains.

The road meanders through Asso, Lasnigo (with its Romanesque church of Sant Alessandro) and Civenna

to Bellagio, between the 'legs' of the lake.

Bellagio is one of the most attractive of the lakeside resorts with pretty views, narrow streets and elegant villas.

From here rejoin statale 583 and follow it along the lake shore through Nesso and Torno to Como.

The historic buildings here include a Gothic-Renaissance Duomo and aristocratic villas from the 18th to early 20th centuries, when Lake Como was one of Europe's most chic holiday destinations.

From Como take scenic statale 340 along the lake's western shore past Cernobbio, Torrigia and Argegno.

From Sala Argegno you can see Lake Como's only island, Isola Comacina. Next come Ossuccio, whose church of Santa Maria Maddalena has a Gothic bell-tower, and Tremezzo, where the gardens of the Villa Carlotta are particularly spectacular in springtime.

The road from here hugs the lakeshore up to the quieter, wilder reaches of the lake. At the northern tip stay on statale 340 when it turns back south. You can continue back to Lecco on the scenic old, lakeside route, or take the faster, new statale 36, which goes through many tunnels as far as Abbadia Lariana.

Distance 183km (113 miles)
Time A full day without much time for stops
Start/end point Lecco ✚ 4B
Lunch Santo Stefano (€€) ✉ Piazza XI Febbraio 3, Lenno (about 27km/17 miles from Como on statale 340) ☎ 0344 55 434
🚫 Closed Mon

PAVIA

Throughout history, Pavia has been an important centre. As capital of the Lombard kings until 1359, it hosted the coronation of, among others, Charlemagne in 774. During the Middle Ages and the Renaissance its ancient 11th-century university could boast such alumni as Petrarch and Leonardo da Vinci. While the town itself is not short of impressive historic sights, Pavia's main draw lies a few kilometres north. The **Certosa di Pavia** (Charterhouse of Pavia) monastery complex was founded in 1396 although most of the present buildings date from the 15th and 16th centuries. Behind a well-proportioned and exquisitely carved Renaissance facade, the interior is mainly Gothic, adorned with marquetry, frescoes and sculpture. In the first chapel on the left is an altar-piece by Perugino, flanked by works by Bergognone, who also painted frescoes in the transept. Some of the altars include semiprecious stones.

www.turismo.provincia.pv.it; **www.**certosadipavia.it

➕ 3C

Certosa di Pavia

✉ Viale del Monumento ☎ 0382 925 613 🕐 May–Sep Tue–Sun 9–11:30, 2:30–5:30 (Oct–Apr closes at sunset) ✋ Donation 🚉 Certosa station

RIVIERA LIGURE

From Ventimiglia in the west to La Spézia in the east, with Genoa (▶ 86) in the middle, the Ligurian coast is known as the Riviera Ligure. The towns and resorts along this stretch cover a range of

styles and tastes from the fishing-village charm of the Cinque Terre
(► 84), through historic Cervo, Albenga, Rapallo and Portovenere
to the revamped 19th-century aristocratic exuberance of San
Remo. Near the French border is the **Villa Hanbury,** with gardens
of exotic plants first laid out by English botanist Sir Thomas
Hanbury in the 1860s and 1870s. On a peninsula, east of Genoa,
is the chic sailing resort of Portofino.

✚ 2D

Villa Hanbury

✉ Corso Monte Carlo 43, Località Mortola ☎ 0184 229 507 🕓 15 Jun–Sep
daily 9–6; Oct daily 10–6; Nov–Mar daily 10–4; Apr–14 Jun daily 10–5
✋ Expensive 🚌 Buses run hourly from Ventimiglia

TORINO (TURIN)

Turin is the capital of the Italian motor industry. The Fabbrica
Italiana Automobili Torino (FIAT) was founded here in 1899 and
became one of the largest businesses in Europe. Today, having
expanded and bought several other Italian car manufacturers, it
accounts for nearly 80 per cent of the cars made in Italy.
Proprietors, the Agnelli family, also own Italy's most famous
football team, Juventus. Turin is also a city of art and, most
famously, home of the Turin Shroud. It is kept in the Cappella della
Sacra Sindone, next to the 15th-century **Duomo** and, although it is
rarely on display, it continues to attract the faithful. The nearby
Palazzo Reale, former residence of the Savoy royal family, contains
many artistic treasures. Other sights include the Palazzo
dell'Accademia delle Scienze, which houses the Galleria Sabauda
painting collection and the important Egyptian museum; the
facade of the Palazzo Carignano, united Italy's first parliament
building; and the elegant main shopping street, Via Roma.
www.turismotorino.org

➕ 2C ✖ Aeroporto Caselle

Duomo

✉ Piazza San Giovanni ☎ 011 436 1540

HOTELS

CINQUE TERRE
Gianni Franzi (€)

Simple little *pensione* where some rooms have panoramic balconies (but shared bathroom). Good restaurant.

✉ Piazza G Marconi 1, Vernazza ☎ 0187 821 003 🕓 Closed Jan–Mar

CREMONA
Astoria (€)

Family-style hotel in the historic centre. Spacious rooms and a restaurant offering good, home cooking to residents (dinner only).

✉ Via Bordigallo 19 ☎ 0372 461 616

GENOA
Hotel Bristol Palace (€€€)

See page 74.

LAGO DI COMO
Grand Hotel Villa Serbelloni (€€€)

See page 74.

MILAN
Gritti (€€)

Close to the Duomo. Well-equipped rooms, all with bath or shower. Breakfast buffet and garage parking included in price.

✉ Piazza Santa Maria Beltrade 1 ☎ 02 801 056; www.hotelgritti.com

Hotel San Guido (€€)

This traditional hotel, fairly close to the heart of the city, has spacious bedrooms and attractive public areas with antiques.

✉ Via C Farini 1A ☎ 02 655 2261; www.nih.it

PAVIA
Excelsior (€)

You will find functional rooms in this good-value hotel near the station. Continental breakfasts are served at the bar (charge).

✉ Piazza Stazione 25 ☎ 0382 28 596

RIVIERA LIGURE
Hotel Cavour (€€)
In the centre of Rapallo and within walking distance of the sea.
Appetizing Mediterranean cuisine served in the restaurant.
✉ Galleria Raggio 20, Rapallo ☎ 0185 54 040; www.cavourhotel.com

TURIN
Chelsea (€€)
Quiet, welcoming, family-run hotel in a central position near the
Duomo. En-suite rooms and air-conditioning.
✉ Via XX Settembre 79 ☎ 011 436 0100; www.hotelchelsea.it

RESTAURANTS

AOSTA
Trattoria Praetoria (€€)
Specialities at this wood-panelled restaurant include country tarts,
home-made pasta and fine cheeses. Wines by the glass or bottle.
✉ Via Sant'Anselmo 9 ☎ 0165 44 356 🕔 Lunch, dinner. Closed Wed pm, Thu

CINQUE TERRE
Gambero Rosso (€€)
Fish and seafood feature at this fine restaurant, with such dishes
as seafood antipasti and *scampi al sale*.
✉ Piazza Marconi 7, Vernazza ☎ 0187 821 265 🕔 Lunch, dinner. Closed Mon

CREMONA
Porta Mosa (€€)
The *padrone* of this simple *osteria* will help you choose which
wines to drink with his lovingly prepared local food.
✉ Via Santa Maria in Betlem 11 ☎ 0372 411 803 🕔 Lunch, dinner. Closed
Sun, Aug and 26 Dec–6 Jan

GENOA
Gran Gotto (€€€)
Ligurian specialities, with a particular emphasis on fish.
✉ Viale Brigate Bisagno 69r ☎ 010 564 344 🕔 Lunch, dinner. Closed Sat
lunch, Sun, two weeks in Aug

LAGO MAGGIORE
Osteria dell'Angolo (€€)
Overlooking the lakeside promenade, eat freshwater fish and other local specialities washed down with excellent local wines.

✉ Piazza Garibaldi 35, Verbania ☎ 0323 556 362 ⏰ Lunch, dinner. Closed Nov, Sun dinner, Mon. Reservations advisable

MILAN
Sadler (€€€)
Claudio Sadler's talent shines at this famous restaurant, where the menu changes with the seasons, but the dishes are consistently creative and modern – the very best of new-wave Italian cooking.

✉ Via Sforza 77 ☎ 02 5810 4451 ⏰ Dinner only. Closed Sun

Trattoria Milanese (€€)
Local specialities, including *risotto alla milanese*.

✉ Via Santa Marta 11 ☎ 02 8645 1991 ⏰ Lunch, dinner. Closed Tue, Jul–end Aug

PAVIA
Antica Osteria del Previ (€€)
It's worth travelling out of central Pavia to taste traditional Pavesi fare such as risotto, and *rane fritte* (fried frogs).

✉ Via Milazzo 65 ☎ 0382 26 203 ⏰ Lunch (not summer) and dinner. Closed early Jan and Aug

TURIN
Montagna Viva (€–€€)
Set menus at varying prices offer the finest local specialities. Hams, mountain lamb and more than 100 cheeses are complemented by a superb wine list.

✉ Piazza Emanuele Filiberto 3 ☎ 011 521 7882 ⏰ Lunch, dinner Mon–Fri, Sat lunch only

SHOPPING

FASHION AND ACCESSORIES

Armani

✉ Via Manzoni 31, Milan ☎ 02 7231 8600

Dolce e Gabbana

✉ Via della Spiga 26a, Milan ☎ 02 7600 1155

Mandarina Duck

✉ Via Orefici 10, Milan ☎ 02 8646 2198

Prada

✉ Via Montenapoleone 6/8, Milan ☎ 02 777 1771

Versace

✉ Via Montenapoleone 11, Milan ☎ 02 7600 8528

ENTERTAINMENT

NIGHTLIFE

Alcatraz

One of Milan's largest clubs, the Alcatraz rocks with live music and disco until well after 4am. It only really gets going after midnight. Dress to impress.

✉ Via Valtellina 25, Milan ☎ 02 6901 6352

Docks Dora

An urban setting for alternative music, cinema, and other performances.

✉ Via Valprato 68, Turin ☎ 011 280 251, 011 248 1139

Hollywood

The place to people-watch, frequented by models, sports people and big names from the Milan fashion scene.

✉ Corso Como 15, Milan ☎ 02 655 5318; www.discotecahollywood.com

NOISE
The best place for local and visiting DJs in Turin, as well as some interesting visiting bands.

✉ Via San Massimo 1, Turin ☎ 011 883 322

Plastic
Open till late with Milan's best DJs and a loyal, vaguely alternative clientele.

✉ Viale Umbria 120, Milan ☎ 02 733 996

Shocking Club
Avant-garde venue for garage, hip-hop, house and underground, where Milan's sophisticated youth come to hang out at weekends.

✉ Via Bastioni di Porta Nuova 12, Milan ☎ 02 657 5073

OPERA, BALLET, THEATRE AND CLASSICAL MUSIC
Piccolo Teatro di Milano
Milan's main theatre, founded in 1947, is one of the best in Italy for traditional productions of Italian and foreign classics (in Italian).

✉ Via Rovello 2, Milan ☎ 02 4241 1889; www.piccoloteatro.org

Teatro alla Scala
The most famous opera house in the world opened its doors in 1778 and has, since then, continued to attract the most sumptuous and (occasionally) original productions and the biggest names of opera. The Museo Teatrale has sets and costumes from La Scala's productions and a good view of the auditorium for those who fail to get their hands on tickets, which are sold out months in advance.

✉ Via Filodrammatici 2, Milan ☎ 02 88791; www.teatroallascala.org.
Museo Teatrale: 02 887 9473

SPORTS AND ACTIVITIES

MOTOR RACING

The Italian Formula One Grand Prix is held at Monza, near Milan, in September.

MOUNTAINEERING, HILLWALKING
Club Alpino Italiano

✉ Via Petrella 19, Milan ☎ 02 205 7231; www.cai.it

SAILING
Federazione Italiana Vela

✉ Piazza Bovgo Pila 40, Genoa ☎ 010 544 541; www.federvela.it

SKIING

In winter you are never very far from a ski resort. The best areas are in the north, particularly Val D'Aosta and the Dolomites. Local tourist offices can tell you where to go and how to get there or try Federazione Italiana Sport Invernali ✉ Via Peranesi 44b, 20137 Milan ☎ 02 75 731; www.fisi.org

SOCCER

Soccer is followed with a passion in Italy. You can always tell when an important game is underway just by listening to the cheers and roars coming form the houses in the street and the animated crowds watching a television screen in a bar. Needless to say, the atmosphere at the stadium is particularly exciting and anybody with any interest in soccer at all should try to attend a match (buy tickets in advance).

Inter Milan and AC Milan (both teams)

✉ Stadio San Siro, Via Piccoliminni 5, Milan ☎ 02 4001 1228; www.inter.it; www.acmilan.it

Juventus (Turin)

✉ Stadio delle Alpi, Strada Altessano 131, Continassa, Venaria Reale, Turin ☎ 011 569 8485; www.juventus.it

Northeast Italy

**Most people come to northeast Italy
to see Venice, whose magnetic
charm attracts about 12 million
tourists every year. However,
there are plenty of other things to
see and do in this scenically varied
area, which stretches from the majestic,
rocky Dolomites to the seemingly unending flatness
of the Po Valley.**

Venezia

For a start, the area's cuisine, particularly that of the Emilia-
Romagna region, is renowned throughout Italy. Medieval
prosperity, often based on trade with the East, has left a heritage
of churches and imposing civic buildings. They complement the
stately palaces, elegant villas and priceless art collections of
the powerful families and prince-bishops who ruled the area
throughout much of its history and attracted some of the greatest
artistic and architectural geniuses of all time.

VENEZIA (VENICE)

One of the most painted, filmed and written about cities in the world, Venice is disturbingly beautiful; nothing quite prepares you for that first glimpse of distant domes and spires emerging from the flat, grey waters like a mirage. Within the city, murky canal water laps the bases of dreamlike buildings, creating a slightly disorienting, rocking effect enhanced by the gentle rattle of the wind in boats and mooring poles.

✚ 7C

ℹ Piazza San Marco 71F ☎ 041 529 8711; www.turismovenezia.it

Accademia, Galleria dell'

This is the place to see Venetian art from the 14th to 18th centuries. While 14th-century artists (such as the Veneziano

brothers) reflect the Byzantine and International Gothic movements that swept Europe, from the Renaissance onwards Venetian artists (such as Giorgione, Lotto, Titian, Tintoretto and Veronese) developed a style that made greater use of colour and softer, more sensuous lines than their contemporaries elsewhere were using.

www.gallerieaccademia.org

✉ Campo della Carità ☎ 041 522 2247; advance reservations 041 520 0345
🕐 Tue–Sun 8:15–7:15, Mon 8:15–2. Closed 1 Jan, 1 May, 25 Dec ✋ Expensive

Ca' d'Oro (Golden House)

Regarded as the most beautiful *palazzo* in Venice, the lacy, Gothic facade of this stately residence (built 1420–34), used to be richly decorated with gold leaf and other luxurious materials. Now it houses the Galleria Giorgio Franchetti, the musician's spectacular collection of sculpture, tapestry and painting.

www.cadoro.org

✉ Calle Ca' d'Oro ☎ 041 522 2349
🕐 Tue–Sun 8:15–7:15, Mon 8:15–2. Closed 1 Jan, 1 May, 25 Dec ✋ Inexpensive

Madonna dell'Orto

Inside this 15th-century Gothic church, tucked away in a corner of Cannaregio, are the tomb of the painter Tintoretto and some fine examples of his work. Most noteworthy of the paintings are a dramatic *Last Judgement* (to the right of the chancel) and an *Adoration of the Golden Calf*, on the left.

✉ Campo Madonna dell'Orto ☎ 041 275 0462; www.chorusvenezia.org
🕐 Mon–Sat 10–5, Sun 1–5 ✋ Inexpensive

Piazza San Marco
Best places to see, ➤ 48–49.

Santa Maria Gloriosa dei Frari
This enormous Gothic church is packed with masterpieces by famous artists. Among them are a Donatello statue of John the Baptist (1450) to the right of the altar, a Bellini altarpiece in the sacristy, Titian's *Assumption of the Virgin* (1518) above the main altar, and Pietro Lombardo's carved rood-screen (1475). Among the many tombs and memorials are Canova's surprising pyramidical tomb (1822), based on one of his own designs, and a memorial to Titian.

✉ Campo dei Frari ⏰ Mon–Sat 9–6, Sun and public hols 1–6 ☎ 041 275 0462 ✋ Inexpensive

Santi Giovanni e Paolo
Also known as San Zanipolo, this severe 14th-century Dominican church made the perfect setting for the Doges' funerals. They were held here from 1450 and the church contains many of their tombs. Among the most interesting are those by Pietro Lombardo,

especially the arched tomb of Andrea Vendramin (1476–78), to the left of the altar. Other gems here include a magnificent polyptych by Bellini (1465), to the right of the entrance, and works by Veronese. The equestrian statue of Bartolomeo Colleoni (1480s) in the piazza outside is by Andrea Verrocchio.

✉ Campo Santi Giovanni e Paolo ☎ 041 523 5913
🕐 Daily 7:30–6:30 ✋ Inexpensive

Scuola Grande di San Rocco

Anyone with any interest in Tintoretto should visit this building, erected between 1515 and 1549 to house a charitable religious order. Its two floors contain more than 50 Tintoretto paintings executed from 1564 to 1587, including some of his greatest works, such as the sombre *Crucifixion* (1565) and eight scenes from the *Life of the Virgin* (1583–87). There are a few works by other artists, including Titian and the sculptor Francesco Pianta, whose caricature bust of Tintoretto in the upper hall is recognisable from the master's own self-portrait at the entrance to the Sala dell'Albergo.

www.scuolagrandesanrocco.it
✉ Campo San Rocco ☎ 041 523 4864 🕐 Apr–Oct daily 9–5:30; Nov–Mar daily 10–5. Closed 1 Jan, Easter, 25 Dec ✋ Expensive; free 16 Aug (Saint's Day)

a boat trip

around the Isole Venezia

The Venetian lagoon is scattered with islands, some uninhabited, some holding ruinous buildings that once housed hospitals and monasteries, some privately owned. In the northern waters, the three islands of Murano, Burano and Torcello have been populated for centuries and are high on most tourists' excursion list.

The vaporetto from Piazzale Roma heads down the Grand Canal and north up the Canale di Cannaregio to the open lagoon. It crosses the water towards Murano, passing the Isola di San Michele.

This island has been used as a cemetery since 1807, though its lovely Renaissance church dates from 1469. Diaghilev, Stravinsky and Ezra Pound are among those who lie behind its protective walls.

North of here is the island of Murano.

The centre of Venetian glass-blowing since the 13th century, Murano has numerous *fornace*, offering guided tours, and the Museo del Vetro, which traces the history of glass manufacture since Roman times.

A further 35 minutes by boat is the island of Burano.

A traditional fishing and lace-making centre, Burano's main draws are its picturesque, brightly coloured houses and the church of San Martino, with its leaning tower and *Crucifixion* by Tiepolo.

Torcello, the last island, is the most historic.

Torcello, settled in the 5th century, once housed a thriving population of more than 20,000 and had fine houses and numerous canals. Malaria in the 14th century caused the inhabitants to flee, and now all that remains are the 9th- to 11th-century Basilica di Santa Maria Assunta, the oldest building in Venice, and the 12th-century church of Santa Fosca. The basilica, lofty, serene and bare, has superb Byzantine mosaics on the vaults and walls, while Santa Fosca, with its Greek-cross plan and external colonnade, exudes age-old peace and sanctity.

Distance 20km (12.5 miles)
Time Allow most of a day
Start/end point Piazzale Roma
Lunch Al Gatto Nero (€€) ⊠ Fondamenta della Giudecca 88, Burano ☎ 041 730 120 🕓 Closed Mon
Locanda Cipriani (€€€) ⊠ Piazza Santa Fosca 29, Torcello ☎ 041 730 150 🕓 Closed Tue and Jan

More to see in Northeast Italy

BOLOGNA

The capital of Emilia-Romagna is a cultured, prosperous city of
arcaded streets and historic monuments. It has one of the oldest
universities in Europe (13th century or earlier), which numbers the
inventor of radio, Guglielmo Marconi, among its alumni. In the
heart of Bologna is the Piazza del Nettuno, with a magnificent
Neptune fountain (1566) sculpted by Giambologna. The Basilica di
San Petronio (started in 1390) has a spacious, calm interior with

high, vaulted ceilings and exquisite biblical bas-relief doors (1425–38) by Jacopo della Quercia. Opposite is the Renaissance Palazzo del Podestà. To the east are two 12th-century *torri pendenti* (leaning towers), survivors of the nearly 200 towers built in the Middle Ages by local nobles. The nearby church of **San Giacomo Maggiore** contains the magnificent chapel of the Bentivoglio family, with frescoes, paintings and della Quercia's Bentivoglio tomb (1435). The **Pinacoteca Nazionale** has in its important collection works by Bolognese painters Guido Reni, Guercino and the Carracci. Also worth a visit is the **Abbazia di Santo Stefano,** a complex of four medieval churches dating for the most part from the 11th century.

🚹 6D 🛪 Aeroporto Marconi

San Giacomo Maggiore

✉ Piazza Verdi a Rossini ☎ 051 225 970 🕐 Apr–Oct daily 10–1, 3–7; Nov–Mar daily 10–1, 2–8 ✋ Donation

Pinacoteca Nazionale

✉ Via delle Belle Arti 56 ☎ 051 420 9411; www.pinacotecabologna.it 🕐 Tue–Sun 9–6:30. Closed Mon and public hols ✋ Moderate

Abbazia di Santo Stefano

✉ Via Santo Stefano ☎ 051 223 256; www.abbaziasantostefano.it 🕐 Mon–Sat 9–12, 3:30–6; Sun and public hols 9–1, 3:30–6:30

BRESSANONE

Known as Brixen by its German-speaking population, this delightful medieval Alpine town lies on the road to Austria. Until 1803 it was ruled by a prince-bishop, whose sumptuous palace (rebuilt in 1595 over a 14th-century original) now houses a museum of art and local history. The 18th-century Duomo has a beautiful 13th-century cloister with 15th-century frescoes.

www.brixen.org

🚹 6A

ℹ Via Stazione 9 ☎ 0472 836 401

DOLOMITI (DOLOMITES)

Right up in the north of Italy, nestling under Austria, is the German-speaking Alto Adige (or Südtirol), much of it covered by the Dolomite mountains. Although this is Italy, the language, scenery, architecture and much of the culture are strongly influenced by Austria, and nearly all the place names have versions in German.

The capital of Alto Adige is Bolzano (or Bozen), which has a fine 15th-century Gothic Duomo, and the **Museo Archeologico dell'Alto Adige,** whose highlight is the 5,300-year-old mummified corpse of what was probably a murder victim. To the west of this is a string of mountain resorts from which cable-cars carry skiers in winter, hillwalkers in summer and view-seekers all year round up into the mountains.

www.bolzano-bozen.it

➕ 6B 🚉 To Bolzano, then buses to other centres

Museo Archeologico dell'Alto Adige

✉ Via Museo 43, Bolzano ☎ 0471 320 100; www.archaeologiemuseum.it 🕒 Jul–Aug, Dec daily 10–5:30; Jan–Jun, Sep–Nov Tue–Sun 10–5:30. Closed 1 Jan, 1 May, 25 Dec ✋ Expensive

FERRARA

This evocative old walled town, ruled by the rich and powerful Este family for centuries, is slightly off the beaten tourist track. The historic centre, with its Renaissance grid layout, contains some marvellous buildings. Chief among these are a 12th-century Duomo with a spectacular arched facade showing scenes from the Last Judgement, and **Castello Estense** (started 1385), the fairytale moated seat of the Este family, whose rivals were left to rot in its chilling dungeons. Among the most beautiful *palazzi* are Palazzo Schifanoia, another Este residence, started in 1385 and with murals by local painters, and **Palazzo dei Diamanti,** now an art gallery and museum. In winter, dense white mists rise up from the nearby River Po and smother the entire area.

➕ 6D

ℹ Castello Estense ☎ 0532 299 303

Castello Estense

✉ Largo Castello 🕐 Tue–Sun 9–5:30. Closed 25 Dec ✋ Moderate

Palazzo dei Diamanti

✉ Corso Ercole I d'Este 21 ☎ 0532 205 844 🕐 Tue, Wed, Fri 9–2, Thu, Sat 9–7, Sun 9–1 ✋ Moderate

MANTOVA (MANTUA)

The beautiful city of Mantua, surrounded on three sides by water, is approached through dreary 20th-century suburbs. Persevere, and you'll find yourself in a wonderfully preserved city, which was once home to one of Europe's most glittering Renaissance courts. Three lovely, interlocking squares lie at its heart, one of which is home to the **Palazzo Ducale,** seat of the Gonzagas, whose frescoed portraits by local painter Mantegna (1431–1505) can be seen in the Camera degli Sposi. The same family's **Palazzo del Tè** was designed and sumptuously decorated by Giulio Romano in 1525–35. Romano was also responsible for the stuccoes inside the Duomo, while the facade of the Basilica di Sant'Andrea is the work of the pioneer Renaissance architect Alberti (1404–72).

www.turismo.mantova.it

➕ 5C

ℹ Piazza Mantegna 6 ☎ 0376 432 432

Palazzo Ducale

✉ Piazza Sordello 40 ☎ 0376 352 100; www.mantovaducale.it 🕐 Tue–Sun 8:45–7:15. Closed 1 Jan, 1 May, 25 Dec ✋ Expensive

Palazzo del Tè

✉ Viale Tè ☎ 0376 323 266 🕐 Tue–Sun 10–6, Mon 1–6 ✋ Expensive

MODENA

Founded as the Roman colony of Mutina, Modena has flourished throughout much of its history and is now associated with those symbols of modern prosperity, Ferrari and Maserati cars, which are manufactured in its outskirts. Among the principal sights of its winding medieval streets and pretty piazzas is a particularly fine Romanesque Duomo (started in 1099), with an 88m-high (288ft) Gothic tower, La Ghirlandina. On its west facade are 12th-century reliefs by Wiligelmo; inside, the rood-screen has scenes from the Passion. Within the **Palazzo dei Musei** is the massive Este Biblioteca (library) of rare, historic manuscripts and the family's collection of works by mainly local artists.

✚ 5D

Palazzo dei Musei

✉ Largo di Porta Sant'Agostino 337 ☎ Galleria: 059 203 3100; Biblioteca: 059 222 248 🕐 Jun–Sep Tue–Fri 9–12, Sat–Sun 10–1, 4–7; Oct–May Tue–Fri 9–12, Sat–Sun 10–1, 3–6. Closed public hols 🖐 Moderate

PADOVA (PADUA)

This stately old university town has a matchless collection of historic and artistic treasures. At the top of the list is the **Cappella degli Scrovegni,** a 14th-century building adorned with Giotto's elegant, soothing frescoes of scenes from the Life of Christ. Reopened in March 2002 after extensive restoration, visitors now have to make reservations in advance (▶ 111). Around the altar of the 13th-century Basilica di Sant'Antonio are Donatello's bronze reliefs of the saint's life (1444). The Donatello statue of the *condottiere* (mercenary soldier) Gattamelata, outside, was the first equestrian statue of the Renaissance. Other gems include the

Chiesa and Museo degli Eremitani, both packed with priceless Renaissance art and historic artefacts, including two frescoes by Mantegna, the only ones to survive a bombing raid in 1944; the 16th-century anatomy theatre in the University's Palazzo del Bo; Titian's first known works in the Scuola del Santo; and the 16th-century Duomo, designed in part by Michelangelo.

www.padovanet.it; **www.**turismopadova.it

✚ 6C

Cappella degli Scrovegni

✉ Piazza Eremitani ☎ 049 201 0020; www.cappelladegliscrovegni.it

🕓 Advance booking required, by phone (3 days in advance) or online the day before. Closed public hols ⬛ Expensive

PARMA

Not only is Parma one of the eating capitals of Italy, but it also has some fine buildings and works of art. The main cupola of the Romanesque Duomo is covered with Correggio's *Assumption* (1534), while in the south transept is a 12th-century frieze showing the Descent from the Cross. Perpendicular to the Duomo is an exquisite 16-sided baptistery (1196, by Benedetto Antelami), with 13th-century reliefs and frescoes depicting the Life of Christ. The

Galleria Nazionale has a fine collection of 14th- to 18th-century art.

www.turismo.comune.parma.it

✚ 4D

Galleria Nazionale

✉ Piazzale della Pilotta 9A ☎ 0521 233 309 🕓 Tue–Sun 9–2. Closed 1 Jan, 1 May, 25 Dec ⬛ Expensive

RAVENNA

Best places to see, ➤ 52–53.

RIMINI

Rimini's vibrant seafront hides an interesting and attractive historic centre which is based around Piazza Cavour and the 14th-century Palazzo del Podestà. The most important monument is the church, the Tempio Malestiano, designed in 1450 by Renaissance architect Leon Battista Alberti, with frescoes by Piero della Francesca.

www.riminiturismo.it

⊞ 7E

TRENTO

This attractive town is surrounded by mountains. Its Romanesque-Gothic Duomo was where the Council's decrees were proclaimed. Piazza del Duomo contains the medieval Palazzo Pretorio and some 16th-century frescoed houses. The magnificent **Castello del Buonconsiglio** has frescoes by Romanino and others, and houses part of the province's art collection.

⊞ 6B

Castello del Buonconsiglio

✉ Via Bernardo Clesio 5 ☎ 0461 233 770 🕓 Jun–Oct Tue–Sun 10–6; Nov–May Tue–Sun 9:30–5. Closed 1 Jan, 1 May, 25 Dec 💰 Moderate

TREVISO

Treviso's walled centre is full of meandering streets and graceful canals. The medieval and Renaissance buildings of Piazza dei Signori include the church of Santa Lucia, with frescoes by Tommaso da Modena (14th century). Gothic San Nicolò contains more da Modena frescoes, as well as works by Lorenzo Lotto and others, while the 15th- to 16th-century Duomo has a Titian altarpiece and an 11th-century baptistery. There is good Renaissance art in the **Museo Civico.**

⊞ 7C

Museo Civico

✉ Borgo Cavour 24 ☎ 0422 658442 🕓 Tue–Sat 9–12:30, 2:30–5, Sun 9–12. Closed public hols 💰 Inexpensive

TRIESTE

Trieste is built on the coast, with most of its hinterland in Slovenia. It has a long maritime tradition and among its places of interest are the Museo del Mare, which traces the history of seafaring. In the town centre is the fascinating Duomo San Giusto, a 14th-century building linking two 5th-century basilicas that contains spectacular 12th-century mosaics. The splendid 15th- to 16th-century **Castello di San Giusto,** with wonderful views, houses a museum with a good weapons and armour collection.

www.triestetourism.it

✚ 8C

🛈 Piazza Unità d'Italia 14 ☎ 040 347 8312

Castello di San Giusto

✉ Piazza Cattedrale 3 ☎ 040 308 686 🕓 Apr–Sep daily 9–7; Oct–Mar daily 9–5. Closed public hols 💷 Inexpensive

UDINE

This pretty, hilly town has excellent views over Friuli towards the Alps from the 16th-century Castello. The Piazza della Libertà contains the Porticato di San Giovanni with its 1527 clocktower. The nearby Arco Bollani was designed by Palladio (1556). The artist Giambattista Tiepolo (1696–1770) was very active in Udine and his works grace the **Palazzo Arcivescovile** (Archbishop's Palace), the Musei Civici and the 14th-century Duomo.

✚ 8B

Palazzo Arcivescovile

✉ Via Treppo 7 ☎ 0432 414 511 🕐 Tue–Sun 10–5 ✋ Moderate

VERONA

Verona attracts visitors to its 1st-century BC **Roman arena** for outdoor opera in summer. Among other important monuments is the church of **San Zeno Maggiore** (1123–35). Bronze door panels (11th and 12th century) depict scenes from the Bible and the life of San Zeno, while the interior's highlights include a ship's keel ceiling (1376) and an altarpiece by Mantegna (1450s). The two main squares are the Piazza dei Signori, with the 12th-century Palazzo del Comune (town hall), and the Piazza delle Erbe, with a busy market. The Scaligeri family, who governed the town from 1260 to 1387, are commemorated by a 14th-century bridge leading to the **Castelvecchio,** and by the Arche Scaligere, their opulent tombs.

www.tourism.verona.it

✚ 5C

Roman arena

✉ Piazza Brà ☎ 045 800 3024 🕐 Jul–Aug daily 9–3:30; Sep–Jun Mon 1:45–6:30, Tue–Sun 8:30–6:30 (closed during opera performances ✋ Moderate

San Zeno Maggiore

✉ Piazza San Zeno 🕐 Mon–Sat 8:30–6, Sun 1–6. Closed during services

Castelvecchio

✉ Corso Castelvecchio 2 ☎ 045 806 2611 🕐 Tue–Sun 8:30–7:30, Mon 1:45–7:30. Closed public hols ✋ Moderate

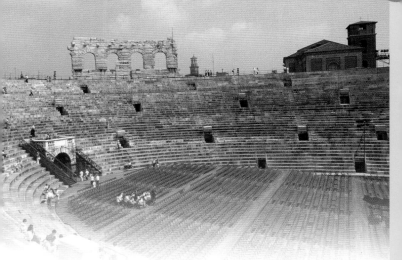

VICENZA

This genteel, gracious city is rich in the works of its most illustrious son, the architect Andrea Palladio (1508–80). Most famous of these is the villa **La Rotonda,** outside the city, which has been copied all over the world. His first public commission was the double-colonnaded Basilica in Piazza dei Signori, where he also designed the Loggia del Capitaniato. Among his other buildings are the Teatro Olimpico (1579), the oldest covered theatre in Europe, and many of the *palazzi* on the Corso Andrea Palladio. The Museo Civico (in another Palladio building) has splendid Gothic and Renaissance art, while older monuments include the Gothic churches of Santa Corona and San Lorenzo and some of the buildings on Contrà Porti, untouched by Palladio.

www.ascom.vi.it

✚ 6C

ℹ Piazza Matteotti 12 ☎ 0444 320 854

La Rotonda

✉ Via Rotonda 45 (about 2km/1.2 miles from Vicenza) ☎ 0444 321 793

🕓 Mid-Mar to Oct: gardens Tue–Sun 10–12, 3–6; interior Wed 10–12, 3–6. Nov to mid-Mar: gardens Tue–Sun 10–12, 2:30–5 ✋ Expensive

HOTELS

BOLOGNA
Art Hotel Bologna (€€)
This excellent hotel, in a 17th-century *palazzo*, has very comfortable rooms – ask for one overlooking Piazza Maggiore.
✉ Via IV Novembre 10 ☎ 0517 457 411; www.bolognarthotels.it

DOLOMITES
Stadt-Città (€€)
Expect modern and elegant rooms with an art deco theme in this beautifully converted 19th-century hotel.
✉ Piazza Walther 21, Bolzano ☎ 0471 975 221; www.hotelcitta.info

PADUA
Milano (€€)
Close to the city centre; popular with business people.
✉ Via P Bronzetti 62 ☎ 0498 712 555; www.hotelmilano-padova.it

PARMA
Button (€)
The entrance and some of the mainly spacious bedrooms have antique furniture. Most rooms have showers, the others baths.
✉ Via Salina 7 ☎ 0521 208 039

RIMINI
Biancamano (€€)
Spacious, comfortable rooms, a good restaurant, and breakfast buffet, which is included in the price.
✉ Via Cappellini 1 ☎ 0541 55491; www.maximilianshotels.it/biancamano

VENICE
Gritti Palace (€€€)
See page 75.

Molino Stucky Hilton (€€€)
Venice's newest, slickest and most international hotel is housed in a superbly converted ex-flour mill on the island of Giudecca.
✉ Giudecca 810 ☎ 041 272 3311; www.hilton.com/venice

VERONA
Bologna (€€)
A 13th-century building near the Arena with comfortable rooms, all with bathrooms. Excellent restaurant.
✉ Piazzetta Scalette Rubiani 3 ☎ 045 800 6830; www.hotelbologna.vr.it

RESTAURANTS

BOLOGNA
La Farfalla (€)
Excellent value by Bolognese standards in former red-light district.
✉ Via Bertiera 12 ☎ 051 225 6560 🕐 Lunch, dinner. Closed Sat dinner (in summer), Sun, two weeks Aug, Christmas

DOLOMITES
Vögele (€€)
The upstairs restaurant serves refined versions of the wide range of Alto Adige dishes offered in the downstairs *osteria*.
✉ Via Goethe 3, Bolzano ☎ 0471 973 938 🕐 Lunch, dinner. Closed Sun, public hols, two weeks Jul

FERRARA
Antica Trattoria Volano (€)
Local culinary masterpieces in one of Ferrara's oldest *trattorie* (18th century).
✉ Via Volano 20 ☎ 0532 761 421 🕐 Lunch, dinner. Closed Fri

MODENA
Erba del Re (€€€)
A modern take on local cooking is the style at this fine restaurant – try one of the tasting menus. Superb wines by the glass.
✉ Via Castel Maraldo 45 ☎ 0592 18188 🕐 Lunch, dinner. Closed Sun and lunchtime Mon; period in Jan and Aug

EXPLORING

PADUA
L'Anfora (€)
A massive range of dishes (including vegetarian), accompanied by a vast selection of wines. Open all afternoon.

✉ Via dei Soncin 13 ☎ 049 656 629 🕐 Lunch, dinner. Closed Sun, Aug

PARMA
Trattoria dei Corrieri (€€)
The menu includes a good range of Parma ham, salami and excellent *parmigiano* cheese.

✉ Via Conservatorio 1 ☎ 0521 234 426 🕐 Lunch, dinner. Closed Sun

RAVENNA
Ca' de' Vén (€)
Wine bar with particularly good regional soups.

✉ Via Ricci 24 ☎ 0544 30 163 🕐 Lunch, dinner (open early for both). Closed Mon, Christmas to mid-Jan, one month in summer

RIMINI
Osteria de Borg (€€)
Cappelletti in brodo is among the best of a range of fresh pasta dishes. Good *menù degustazione* (tasting menu).

✉ Via Forzieri 12 ☎ 0541 56 071 🕐 Lunch, dinner. Closed Mon, 15–30 Jan

TRENTO
Al Vo' (€€)
The menu concentrates on local food, especially cheeses, meats and salami, which can also be bought to take out.

✉ Vicolo del Vo' 11 ☎ 0461 985 374 🕐 Lunch (dinner Thu and Fri only). Closed Sun and late Jun

TREVISO
Toni del Spin (€)
The day's specials may include (according to the season) soups, tripe and pheasant. There is also a good-value wine list.

✉ Via Inferiore 7 ☎ 0422 543 829 🕐 Lunch, dinner. Closed Sun, Mon lunch, Aug

TRIESTE
Buffet da Siora Rosa (€–€€)
Family-run, traditional, all-day Trieste buffet, with a wide range of substantial local dishes.

✉ Piazza Hortis 3 ☎ 040 301 460 🕔 8–8. Closed Sat, Sun, mid-Sep to mid-Oct

VENICE
Alla Madonna (€€)
This famous, bustling restaurant serves the full range of Venetian specialities, with the accent firmly on fish.

✉ San Polo 594, Calle della Madonna ☎ 041 522 3824 (no reservations) 🕔 Lunch, dinner. Closed Wed

Antico Giardinetto (€€)
See page 58.

VERONA
Al Calmiere (€€)
Well-run restaurant offering the best of simple, satisfying Verona cuisine. Outside eating in summer overlooking the busy piazza.

✉ Piazza San Zeno 10 ☎ 045 803 0765 🕔 Lunch, dinner. Closed Wed dinner, Thu, 1st two weeks Jan

VICENZA
Cinzia e Valerio (€€)
Reservations recommended at this popular restaurant serving the best of Veneto's cuisine, especially seafood.

✉ Piazzetta Porta Padova 65 ☎ 0444 505 213 🕔 Lunch, dinner. Closed Sun dinner, Mon, Aug, Christmas–New Year

SHOPPING

CRAFTS, GIFTS AND SOUVENIRS
Ebrû
Beautiful handmade paper made into notebooks, folders, photo frames and boxes in a choice of marbled or stamped paper.

✉ San Marco 3471, Campo Santo Stefano, Venice ☎ 041 523 8830

Mondo Novo

Some of the most unusual and spectacular masks in Venice, made for masked balls and parties during *Carnevale*.

✉ Rio Terrà Canal, Dorsoduro 3063, Venice ☎ 041 528 7344

FOOD AND DRINK

Pasticceria Marchini

Venice's best *pasticceria* has a massive selection of traditional cakes, chocolates and other confectionery.

✉ Spaderia, San Marco 676, Venice ☎ 041 522 9109

ENTERTAINMENT

NIGHTLIFE

Florian

Café founded on Piazza San Marco by Florian Francesconi in 1720; a pianist plays soothing music as you sip extortionately priced drinks in unique surroundings.

✉ Piazza San Marco 56, Venice ☎ 041 520 5641

Harry's Bar

The most famous bar in Italy, founded in 1931, has been frequented by generations of Venice's famous visitors. It's still *the* place for cocktails, but the restaurant is a bit overpriced.

✉ Calle Vallaresso 1323, Venice ☎ 041 528 5777

Paradiso Perduto

Arty bar-cum-eatery with regular live music.

✉ Fondamenta della Misericordia 2540, Venice ☎ 041 720 581

OPERA

Teatro la Fenice

Venice's beautifully rebuilt opera house reopened in 2004; reserve in advance for performances or take a guided tour of the stunning interior.

✉ Campo San Fantin, San Marco 1965, Venice ☎ 041 2424 (box office); www.teatrolafenice.it

Tuscany and Northern Central Italy

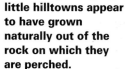

Firenze

Populated by the highly cultured Etruscans centuries before the Romans rose to power, this is an area where rural and urban beauty blend harmoniously. While the landscape seems almost to have been sculpted by the Renaissance artists whose works are everywhere, the little hilltowns appear to have grown naturally out of the rock on which they are perched.

Travellers have been flocking to central Italy for centuries to enjoy the way of life that comes with a pleasant climate, excellent food and wines and an unequalled quantity and quality of art and architecture. For many this is quintessential Italy and, although you will have to share its spectacular sights with many others, the quiet confidence that comes from a long and prosperous history imbues even the busiest piazza with a soothing calm and a sense of continuity.

FIRENZE (FLORENCE)

Florence is Renaissance Italy at its civilized best. The most accomplished artists and architects of the period flocked to Florence from all over central Italy to work for the powerful families. Today, the compact historic centre of Tuscany's busy capital is a mass of masterpieces from that flourishing era.

✚ 5E

ℹ️ Via Cavour 1 ☎ 055 290 832; www.firenzeturismo.it; www.firenze.net

Duomo and Battistero

The Duomo's lavish exterior includes Giotto's 85m-high (278ft) campanile (1334) and reliefs by Pisano and Lucca della Robbia.

The massive dome (1465), by Brunelleschi, was the largest of its time. The facade is 19th-century. Inside are intricate marble inlaid floors (16th-century), Vasari frescoes in the dome, and works by Lucca della Robbia, Ghiberti, Uccello and others. There's more art in the Museo dell'Opera del Duomo (Mon–Sat 9–7:30, Sun 9–1:40). The nearby baptistery has splendid carved doors by Ghiberti and Pisano (Mon–Sat 12–7, Sun 8:30–2).

www.duomofirenze.it

✉ Piazza del Duomo ☎ 055 230 2885

🕐 Duomo: Mon–Wed, Fri 10–5, Thu 10–3:30, Sat 10–4:45, Sun 1:30–4:45; Dome: Mon–Fri 8:30–7, Sat 8:30–5:40. Campanile: daily 8:30–7:30; (last entry 45 mins before closing). Reduced hours first Sat of each month. Closed religious hols ✋ Duomo: free; Campanile and Dome: moderate 🚌 1, 11, 17, 23a

Galleria dell'Accademia

Modern Europe's first art school, the Accademia delle Belle Arti, was founded here in 1563, and many of its original exhibits were acquired for the students to study and copy. Today the main pull of this collection of 15th- to 19th-century Tuscan art is the Michelangelo sculpture, including the original of his seductive *David* (1504), created for Piazza della Signoria (➤ 126), where a copy now stands. Among the other outstanding exhibits here are the four bound *Slaves or Prisoners* (unfinished, 1521–23) by Michelangelo, meant for the tomb of Pope Julius II.

www.accademia.firenze.it; **www.**firenzemusei.it/accademia

✉ Via Ricasoli 60 ☎ 055 238 8612 🕐 Tue–Sun 8:15–6:50. Closed public hols ✋ Expensive 🚌 Many routes

Galleria degli Uffizi
Best places to see, ➤ 46–47.

Museo Nazionale del Bargello
This imposing *palazzo* (1255–1345) was the city governor's residence, then from 1574 the police headquarters; public executions were held in its courtyard until 1786. It became one of Italy's first national museums in 1865. What the Uffizi (➤ 46–47) is to Renaissance painting, the Bargello is to sculpture – many of its exhibits came from the same Medici collections. Michelangelo's works include his first freestanding sculpture, *Bacchus* (1497), while other highlights are Donatello's jaunty *David* (1430), bas-reliefs (1402) by Brunelleschi and Lorenzo Ghiberti, and bronzes by Benvenuto Cellini (1500–71).

www.firenzemusei.it/bargello

✉ Via del Proconsolo 4 ☎ 055 294 883 🕐 Mon–Sat, 2nd and 4th Sun of month 8:15–2. Closed public hols 👋 Moderate 🚌 19

Palazzo Medici-Riccardi

Generally acclaimed as the finest example of Florentine Renaissance architecture, the *palazzo* was started in 1444 by Michelozzo for Cosimo Medici the Elder and was the family's home until 1540. Michelangelo may have designed the windows (1517) next to the entrance. In the elegant courtyard are sculptures, and on one of the upper floors is the Cappella dei Magi with frescoes (1459) by Benozzo Gozzoli.

✉ Via Cavour 3 ☎ 055 276 0340. Advance reservations: 055 294 883
🕐 Thu–Tue 9–7. Closed Wed, public hols 🖐 Moderate 🚌 1, 6, 7, 11, 12, 14

Palazzo Pitti and Giardino di Boboli

Possibly designed by Brunelleschi (1458) for the Pitti banking family, this grandiose *palazzo* was their ostentatious attempt to outdo the Medici who, however, were to buy it from the declining Pitti in 1550. It now houses several museums, the most important of which is the Galleria Palatina, where a rich collection of Renaissance masterpieces is hung in frescoed halls. When open, the 17th-century state apartments are well worth seeing, as are the Galleria del Costume's clothes from the 18th to 20th centuries. Next to the *palazzo* are the Boboli Gardens. Laid out for the Medici after 1550, they are a splendid example of 16th- and 17th-century garden design, with much use of water, statues and formal layouts.

✉ Piazza Pitti ☎ 055 238 8614 🕐 Palace: Tue–Sun 8:15–6:50. Gardens: Jun–Aug, 8–6:30; Nov–Feb, 8–4:30; Mar and Sep, 8–6:30; Oct 8–5:30 (closed first and last Mon of month). Times may be subject to change. Closed public hols
🖐 Palace expensive, gardens moderate 🚌 15, 32, 37, 42

Piazza della Signoria

The political and social heart of Florence is an outdoor art gallery with Ammanati's Fontana di Nettuno (1575) and a copy of Michelangelo's *David* (now in the Galleria dell'Accademia, ➤ 123) among the works that stand outside the Loggia dei Lanzi (1382). In the Loggia are Roman statues, Cellini's *Perseus* (1554) and Giambologna's powerful *Rape of the Sabine Women* (1583). The piazza is dominated by the **Palazzo Vecchio** (1332), a monument to civic worthiness puffed out beneath its 94m (308ft) tower. Its imposing rooms are packed with art by Michelangelo, Vasari, Bronzino, Domenico Ghirlandaio and others.

Palazzo Vecchio

✉ Piazza della Signoria ☎ 055 276 8325 🕐 Mon–Wed, Fri–Sun 9–7, Thu 9–2 (summer Mon and Fri 9am–11pm). Closed public hols ✋ Moderate (includes admission to Santa Maria del Carmine ➤ 128) 🚍 9, 23, 31, 32

Ponte Vecchio

Florence's oldest and most charming bridge, with little shops and houses clinging precariously to the sides, was designed by Taddeo Gaddi (Giotto's pupil) in 1345.

✉ Lungarno Archibuscieri 🚍 Many routes

San Lorenzo

The bare, unfinished facade of this Brunelleschi church (1442–46) hides a Renaissance treasure trove. The bronze pulpits are Donatello's (finished by his pupils in 1460), as are the sacristy decorations and doors (1435–43); the staircase, desks and ceiling of the Biblioteca Medicea Laurenziana are by Michelangelo; and a Bronzino fresco (1659) and some spectacular Medici monuments adorn the church.

✉ Piazza di San Lorenzo ☎ 055 216 634 🕐 Mon–Sat 10–5; closed Sun and public hols; Biblioteca: Mon–Sat 8:30–1:30 🖐 Biblioteca: free; Church: inexpensive 🚌 Many routes

San Marco

Founded in the 13th century, the convent of San Marco was extended by Michelozzo in 1437. Some cells and parts of the building are decorated with frescoes by Fra Angelico (1430s and 1440s), including a hauntingly lovely *Annunciation*.

These form part of the Museo di San Marco, along with a collection of other Renaissance masterpieces.

www.firenzemusei.it/sanmarco

✉ Piazza di San Marco ☎ 055 238 8608; advance booking 055 294 883 🕐 Mon–Fri 8:15–1:50; Sat 8:15–6:50, Sun 8:15–7. Closed 1 Jan, 1 May, 25 Dec 🖐 Expensive 🚌 Many routes

Santa Croce

The spacious interior of this Franciscan church (1294 onwards) holds the tombs of Michelangelo, Machiavelli and other Renaissance greats.

The artworks are too numerous to mention, but include Luca della Robbia roundels in Brunelleschi's Cappella dei Pazzi, Giotto frescoes in the Cappelle Bardi and Peruzzi, a Donatello wooden crucifix, and frescoes (including an early night scene) by Taddeo Gaddi.

www.santacroce.firenze.it

✉ Piazza di Santa Croce ☎ 055 246 6105 🕐 Mon–Sat 9:30–5:30, Sun 1–5:30 ✋ Moderate (includes church and museum) 🚌 11, 19, 31, 32

Santa Maria del Carmine

Fortunately the magnificent Cappella Brancacci frescoes survived a fire which badly damaged the rest of the church in the 18th century. The frescoes, depicting the Life of St Peter, were started by Masolino (1420s) and finished by Filippino Lippi (1480), but the bulk of them are by Masolino's pupil, the Renaissance pioneer Masaccio (1401–28). His realism, expressiveness and use of perspective were carefully studied by subsequent artists. Look for the anguished *Adam and Eve Being Expelled from Eden* (to the left of the chapel), and the facial expressions of characters in the other scenes.

✉ Piazza del Carmine ☎ 055 238 2195 🕐 Mon, Wed–Sat 10–5, Sun 1–5. Closed public hols, 7 Jan, 16 Jul ✋ Moderate (includes admission to Palazzo Vecchio ➤ 126) 🚌 15

Santa Maria Novella

Three founders of the Renaissance movement are represented in this beautiful 13th-century church, with its outstanding stained-glass windows: Alberti, with his dramatic black-and-white marble facade (1458); Brunelleschi, with his wooden crucifix; and Masaccio, whose use of perspective in the splendid *Trinity* fresco (1428) was revolutionary for its time. In addition, there are frescoes (1485) by Domenico Ghirlandaio in the Cappella Tornabuoni, while the museum housed in the church's cloisters contains numerous important frescoes, including some by Uccello. These were badly damaged in 1966 when the River Arno flooded.

✉ Piazza di Santa Maria Novella ☎ 055 282 187 🕐 Church: Mon–Thu and Sat 9:30–5, Sun 9–2; Museum: Mon–Sat 9–4:30, Sun 9–1:30 ✋ Inexpensive

More to see in Tuscany and Northern Central Italy

ANCONA

The capital of the province of Le Marche (The Marches) was founded on the Adriatic coast in the 4th or 5th century BC. Survivors from its early history include a fine collection of Hellenic, Etruscan and Roman art and artefacts in the **Museo Archeologico Nazionale delle Marche** and the well-preserved Arco di Traiano (Trajan's Arch, AD115) overlooking the port. Several later historic monuments survived heavy World War II bombing; among these are the 15th-century Loggia dei Mercanti, with a Gothic facade, and 10th-century Santa Maria della Piazza, with floor mosaics from an earlier church on the same site.

✚ 8E

Museo Archeologico Nazionale delle Marche

✉ Palazzo Ferretti, Via Ferretti 6 ☎ 071 202 602; www.archeomarche.it
🕐 Tue–Sun 8:30–7:30. Closed 1 Jan, 1 May, 25 Dec ✋ Moderate

AREZZO

Originally a major Etruscan and Roman centre, Arezzo preserves remains from its ancient past in the **Museo Archeologico** overlooking a 1st-century Roman amphitheatre. Over the years, the city's many illustrious sons have included the poet Petrarch (1304–74), and the artist Giorgio Vasari (1511–74), who built, decorated and lived in **Casa di Vasari.** He also worked on the **Pieve (parish church) di Santa Maria,** in Corso Italia. Arezzo's main crowd-puller is the church of **San Francesco,** with Piero della Francesca's magnificent frescoes (1452–66). These illustrate the life story of Christ's cross from its origins in the Garden of Eden to its final rediscovery and rescue by St Helena, mother of the emperor Constantine. The **Museo d'Arte Medievale e Moderna** has a good collection of 14th- to 19th-century Tuscan art.

www.apt.arezzo.it

➕ 6E

Museo Archeologico

✉ Via Margaritone 10 ☎ 0575 20 882 🕐 Daily 8:30–7:30 ✋ Moderate

Casa di Vasari

✉ Via XX Settembre 55 ☎ 0575 409 050 🕐 Mon, Wed–Sat 9–7, Sun 9–1
✋ Inexpensive

San Francesco

www.pierodellafrancesca.it

✉ Piazza San Francesco ☎ 0575 352 727 (advance booking obligatory by phone or online) 🕐 Mon–Sat 9–6, Sun 1–5:30 (later in summer).
Reservations essential (☎ 0575 352 727) ✋ Moderate

Museo d'Arte Medievale e Moderna

✉ Via di San Lorentino 8 ☎ 0575 409 050 🕐 Tue–Sun 9–7. Closed public hols ✋ Inexpensive

ASCOLI PICENO

The medieval historic centre of this walled town more or less follows the grid street plan of the old Roman Asculum Picenum. At its heart lies Piazza del Popolo, whose highlights are the 13th-century Palazzo dei Capitani del Popolo, the church of San Francesco (1258–1549), and the adjoining Loggia dei Mercanti (1513). On stately old Piazza dell'Arringo there is a 12th-century Duomo, with another Amatrice facade, a Carlo Crivelli polyptych (1473) inside and a splendid 12th-century baptistery.

www.rinascita.it

✚ 13H

ASSISI

Assisi was at the heart of a series of earthquakes that shook central Italy in the autumn of 1997. Some important historic buildings were damaged, including the **Basilica di San Francesco,** St Francis's burial place and Assisi's most important monument. Started in 1228, this magnificent church contained matchless frescoes by Giotto, Cimabue, Lorenzetti and others. A few of these

were virtually destroyed, but have since been magnificently restored. Other monuments include the 12th- and 13th-century Romanesque **Duomo** huddled next to its hefty campanile; the impressively positioned 14th-century castle, the **Rocca Maggiore;** many small churches and the church of **Santa Chiara,** with Giotto-influenced interior frescoes. Assisi's oldest monument, the 1st-century BC Tempio di Minerva (converted into a church), on the attractive Piazza del Comune, escaped the earthquake unscathed.

www.comune.assisi.pg.it; **www.**assisionline.com

➕ 12H

Basilica di San Francesco

✉ Piazza San Francesco ☎ 075 819 001 ⏰ Apr–Oct Mon–Sat 6:30am–6:50pm, Sun 6:30am–7:15pm; Nov–Mar daily 6:30–6 💰 Inexpensive

Duomo

✉ Piazza San Ruffino

Rocca Maggiore

✉ Via Maria delle Rose
⏰ Daily 9 to sunset

Santa Chiara

✉ Piazza Santa Chiara

CORTONA

This perfect example of a Tuscan hilltown was founded by the Etruscans, whose artefacts, along with other ancient remains, can be seen in the **Museo dell'Accademia Etrusca** in the Palazzo Pretorio, one of the late medieval civic buildings on Piazza della Repubblica. The Museo Diocesano, housed in a deconsecrated church, has works by Fra Angelico, Signorelli (who was born in Cortona) and others.

www.cortonaweb.net

➕ 6F

Museo dell'Accademia Etrusca

✉ Piazza Signorelli 19 ☎ 0575 637 235 ⏰ Apr–Sep daily, 10–7; Oct–Mar Tue–Sun 10–5 💰 Moderate

ELBA

Napoleon was exiled on this lush little island after his 1814 abdication. He led a simple life from his country **Villa San Martino,** but an escape attempt led to exile for real on bleak St Helena in the Atlantic Ocean. Apart from enjoying the beautiful bays, cliffs, fishing villages and inland scenery, visitors today can admire the view from 1,000m (3,280ft) Monte Capanne and explore the intriguing museums in Portoferraio and Marciano.

www.aptelba.it

🚩 9H 🚢 from Piombino

Villa San Martino

✉ San Martino ☎ 0565 914 688 🕓 Mon, Wed–Sat 9–7, Sun 9–1. Closed 1 Jan, 25 Dec 🖐 Inexpensive

GUBBIO

Clinging to the lower slopes of Monte Ingino, this enchanting Umbrian town has remained essentially unchanged since the Middle Ages. Along its winding streets of heavy, full-bodied houses are mysterious narrow doorways, evocatively called *porte della morte* (doors of death). The main monuments include the hefty Palazzo dei Consoli (1332), whose Museo Civico has 3rd-century BC Etruscan-inscribed tablets; the Palazzo Ducale (1470), with its fine Renaissance courtyard; the Gothic **Duomo;** and the 13th-century church of **San Francesco,** with frescoes (1404–13) by Ottaviano Nelli. The stage-like, elevated Piazza della Signoria (or Piazza Grande) is on a man-made platform. Every year at the end of May, three vast, wooden 'ceri' (candles), each 4m (13ft) long, are raced by competing teams through Gubbio and up to the church of Sant'Ubaldo on top of 820m (2,690ft) Monte

Ingino. You can see them in the church by climbing the mountain or taking the cable-car from Porta Romana.

www.gubbioweb.it

➕ 7F

ℹ️ APT Via della Repubblica 15

☎ 075 922 0693

Duomo

✉ Via Ducale

San Francesco

✉ Piazza 40 Martiri

MAREMMA

Italy's answer to the Wild West, where *butteri* (cowboys) herd docile horned cattle and stage rodeo shows, lies along the coast of southern Tuscany. The rest of this area of mainland low hills falls within the **Parco Regionale dell'Uccellina,** with marked footpaths and picnic areas. The evocative ruins of defence towers, built by the Medici in the 16th century, overlook the Maremma's wide, undeveloped beaches. To its north lie salt marshes.

➕ 10H 🚂 and 🚌 to Grosseto

Parco Regionale dell'Uccellina

✉ Centro Visite di Alberese ☎ 0564 407 098 🕐 Apr–Sep daily 8–5; Oct–Mar daily 8:30–1:30

ORVIETO

Orvieto sits on top of a volcanic outcrop and is famous for its wine. The Duomo (13th–16th centuries) is one of the finest in Italy, its dazzling facade a mass of mosaics, sculpture and bas-reliefs with modern bronze doors by Emilio Greco (1969). The highlights of the interior are the Cappella Nuova frescoes by Signorelli (1499). Other unmissables in Orvieto include the nearby **Museo Claudio Faina;** the Pozzo di San Patrizio, a 62m-deep (203ft) well (1527) with two staircases spiralling around its side; and the 13th-century Palazzo del Popolo.

www.orvietoturismo.it

➕ 11H

Museo Claudio Faina

✉ Piazza del Duomo 29 ☎ 0763 341 216 🕐 Apr–Sep daily 9:30–6; Oct–Mar Tue–Sun 10–5. Closed 1 Jan, 25–26 Dec ✋ Moderate

PERUGIA

The outskirts of Perugia are a modern, urban sprawl, but the city centre is pure Medieval and Renaissance, focused on the dramatic Piazza IV Novembre and its 13th-century Fontana Maggiore. Also on the piazza are the Palazzo dei Priori (13th century), its inner walls frescoed by Cavallini (1273–1308), Perugino (1445–1523) and others, and the Gothic Cathedral with a baroque doorway. The **Galleria Nazionale d'Umbria** has the region's best collection of 13th- to 18th-century art. Elsewhere in the city, important

monuments include the Museo Archeologico Nazionale dell'Umbria; and the serene Oratorio di San Bernardino (1457–61), with bas-reliefs by Agostino di Duccio.

 12G

Galleria Nazionale d'Umbria

✉ Corso Vannucci 19 ☎ 075 574 1410; www.gallerianazionaleumbria.it 🕐 Daily 8:30–7:30. Closed 1st Mon of month, public hols 🖐 Expensive

PISA

Pisa's most famous landmark, the 54m (177ft) **Leaning Tower (Torre Pendente),** was leaning so much (about 5.5m/18ft) that it was closed to the public from 1990 until 2001 for major restoration. Built between 1173 and 1350 as the Duomo's campanile, it started to lean in 1274. It is one of four dreamlike monuments on the surreally perfect Campo dei Miracoli (Piazza del Duomo). Buscheto started the Duomo in 1064. Inside are a pulpit (1302–11) carved by Pisano and mosaics (1302) by Cimabue. There is another carved pulpit in the Battistero (12th–13th centuries) with Gothic decoration by Pisano. Although the Camposanto cemetery was badly bombed in World War II, traces of its 14th-century frescoes have survived. The Museo Nazionale di San Matteo houses 13th- to 17th-century Tuscan art, notably works by Andrea Pisano; Piazza dei Cavalieri has many Renaissance buildings by Vasari; and Santa Maria della Spina (1230–1323) is a sugary Gothic creation rebuilt on its present site in 1871 to avoid flooding.

www.pisaturismo.it

🔲 4E

Torre Pendente

✉ Campo dei Miracoli ☎ 050 560 547 🕐 Apr–Sep daily 8–8; Mar, Oct daily 9–6:30; Nov–Feb daily 9–5 🖐 Expensive ❓ Buy tickets online or in advance from the ticket office at the tower

PISTOIA

The heart of Pistoia's walled historic centre is Piazza del Duomo, with the 14th-century Gothic Battistero and the 12th- to 13th-century Duomo, both in striped dark and light marble. Inside the Duomo is the silver altar of St James (1287–1456). Further afield lie the churches of Sant'Andrea (12th century), with pulpit and crucifix (1298–1308) by Giovanni Pisano, and San Giovanni Fuorcivitas (12th–14th centuries), on Via Cavour, with a Taddeo Gaddi polyptych and a Luca della Robbia terracotta. The Ospedale del Ceppo, on Piazza Giovanni XXII, has a unique terracotta frieze by Luca's great-nephew, Giovanni della Robbia.
www.pistoia.turismo.toscana.it

 5E

SAN GALGANO

The romantic remains of a 13th-century abbey, dissolved in the 17th century, lie surrounded by lush trees and fields between Siena and Massa Marittima. The abbey was built by Cistercian monks in French Gothic style, and its remains give an insight into how such buildings were constructed. Overlooking the abbey is the circular Cappella di Montesiepi, containing a sword miraculously thrust into rock by St Galgano and frescoes of scenes from the saint's life (1344) by Ambrogio Lorenzetti.

10G 🚌 Bus from Siena

SAN GIMIGNANO

The skyline of San Gimignano, one of the loveliest and most visited medieval hilltowns in Tuscany, is dominated by 13 towers erected in the 12th and 13th centuries. At its heart lie Piazza della Cisterna, with a lovely medieval well, and Piazza del Duomo, where the 12th- to 13th-century **Collegiata** contains magnificent art by Ghirlandaio (1448–94) and others. There is more exceptional early Renaissance art in the Museo Civico, housed in the

13th-century Palazzo del Popolo, whose 54m-high (177ft) tower is the town's tallest. The 13th-century church of Sant'Agostino has frescoes by Benozzo Gozzoli among its impressive artworks.

www.comune.sangimignano.siena.it

➕ 5E

ℹ️ Piazza Duomo 1 ☎ 0577 940 008

Collegiata

✉️ Piazza del Duomo ☎ 0577 942 226 🕐 Mar–Oct Mon–Fri 9:30–7:30, Sat 9:30–5, Sun 1–5; Nov–Feb Mon–Sat 9:30–5, Sun 1–5 ✋ Moderate

SAN MARINO

San Marino, Europe's oldest surviving republic, just 61sq km (24sq miles), is set on a steep hill with commanding views over the surrounding countryside from the battlements of its fortress. Founded in the 4th century and still nominally indpendent, it issues its own currency and postage stamps and enjoys duty-free status, ensuring huge crowds of tourists in search of cut-price bargains.

➕ 7E 🚌 Access by bus

ℹ️ APT Palazzo del Turismo, Contrada Omagnano 20 ☎ 0549 882 410

SIENA

Winding streets of dignified medieval and Renaissance buildings open out on to the main Piazza del Campo, a dramatic, sloping, shell-shaped piazza with the 13th- to 14th-century Palazzo Pubblico at its foot. Inside the palazzo is the **Museo Civico,** whose frescoes of *Good and Bad Government* (Lorenzetti, 1338–40) symbolize the philosophy of this civilized city. Towering over the *palazzo* is the 102m (334ft) Torre del Mangia (1138), with excellent views at the top of its 505 stairs. Every summer competing local teams, each wearing different colours, race horses round the *campo* in the *Palio* (► 25). Behind the opulent facade of the Duomo (1136–1382) lies a wealth of art treasures, including Pinturicchio frescoes (1509) in the Piccolomini Library, a font by della Quercia and Donatello, and a magnificent

marble inlaid floor. The Museo dell'Opera del Duomo, the Ospedale di Santa Maria della Scala and the Pinacoteca Nazionale contain other important artworks. Civic relics from Siena's past are on display in the Palazzo Piccolomini (1460s). Siena's (and one of Italy's) patron saints, St Catherine of Siena (1347–80), dedicated herself to God at the age of eight and became a holy mystic. Her house (Via Camporeggio 37) is full of illustrations of her life while her preserved head is in the church of San Domenico (1226 onwards), along with various frescoes.

www.terresiena.it

➕ 5F

Museo Civico

☎ 0577 226 230 🕓 Daily 10–6:30 ✋ Expensive

SPOLETO

This breathtaking Umbrian town contains relics from a history that dates back to pre-

Roman times. These include the 1st-century BC Arco di Druso (Arch of Drusus), in Piazza del Mercato, and the monumental Ponte delle Torri (Bridge of Towers), built in the 12th century over the remains of a Roman aqueduct. The graceful

facade of the 12th-century **Duomo** has no fewer than eight rose windows; the restored, largely 17th-century interior includes works by Bernini, Pinturicchio and Carracci.

➕ 12H

ℹ APT Piazza della Libertà 7 ☎ 0743 238 920

Duomo

✉ Piazza del Duomo

TODI

Spilling over the edge of its hilltop location, this pretty town is notable for its medieval architecture. Piazza del Popolo, at its heart, is the setting for the 13th-century Palazzo del Capitano, Palazzo del Priori and Palazzo del Popolo, housing the restored **Museo Etrusco-Romano and Pinacoteca** (picture gallery). The regal Romanesque-Gothic Duomo contains fine Renaissance stalls, while the church of San Fortunato is a pleasing mix of Gothic and Renaissance, with frescoes (1432) by Masolino. One of the best gems of the Italian Renaissance, the church of Santa Maria della Consolazione (probably planned by Bramante), lies on the Orvieto road, on the outskirts of Todi.

✚ 12H

ℹ APT Piazza Umberto I, 6 ☎ 075 894 3395

Museo Etrusco-Romano and Pinacoteca

✉ Piazza del Popolo ☎ 075 894 4148 🕐 Apr–Oct daily 10–1:30, 3–6; Nov–Mar daily 10:30–1, 2:30–5 ✋ Moderate

URBINO

The Renaissance genius Raphael (1483–1520) was born here. One of the few works he left to his home town is in the **Galleria Nazionale delle Marche,** in the Renaissance Palazzo Ducale (1444–82), alongside other masterpieces by the likes of Lucca della Robbia, Uccello and Piero della Francesca; the Casa di Raffaello contains only copies of

Raphael's paintings. The Duomo was rebuilt by Valadier after an earthquake in 1789. The oratories of San Giuseppe (16th century) and San Giovanni Battista (late 14th century) are also worth visiting; the first for its fine crib and the second for frescoes (1416) by brothers Giacomo and Lorenzo Salimbeni.

🚼 7E
🛈 APT Piazza Rinascimento 1
☎ 0722 2613

Galleria Nazionale delle Marche
✉ Piazza Duca Federico ☎ 0722 329 057 🕐 Mon 8:30–2, Tue–Sun 8:30–7:15. Closed 1 Jan, 1 May, 25 Dec 💶 Moderate

VOLTERRA

This is one of the best places to see Etruscan remains. These include parts of the Arco Etrusco (the rest is Roman) and the unrivalled **Museo Etrusco Guarnacci**'s collection. There is also a fine 1st-century BC Roman theatre. Other sights include excellent 14th- to 17th-century Tuscan art in the Pinacoteca and Museo Civico; austere 13th-century *palazzi* on Piazza dei Priori; and a Romanesque Duomo, with 13th-century sculpture and baptistery and 12th-century bas-reliefs on the 17th-century pulpit.

www.volterratour.it
🚼 5E

Museo Etrusco Guarnacci
✉ Via Don Minzoni 15 ☎ 0588 86 347 🕐 Mid-Mar to Oct 9–7; Nov to mid-Mar 9–2. Closed 1 Jan, 25 Dec 💶 Expensive (includes entrance to Pinacoteca)

HOTELS

ELBA
Villa Ombrosa (€€)
Many bedrooms have balconies overlooking the beach. Breakfast
(not included) and lunch on the terrace.
✉ Via A de Gasperi 3, Portoferraio ☎ 0565 914 363; www.villaombrosa.it

FLORENCE
Loggiata dei Serviti (€€€)
See page 74.

Orto dei Medici (€€)
In a historic *palazzo* with antique furniture and frescoed walls.
Restored, comfortable rooms. Breakfast buffet included.
✉ Via San Gallo 30 ☎ 055 483 427; www.ortodeimedici.it

GUBBIO
Bosone Palace (€)
Excellent value in a 17th-century *palazzo* with antique furniture in
the individually decorated bedrooms (all with bath).
✉ Via XX Settembre 22 ☎ 075 922 0688

ORVIETO
Grand Hotel Italia (€€)
The rooms are comfortably furnished and many have balconies.
✉ Via del Popolo 13 ☎ 0763 342 065; www.grandhotelitalia.it

PERUGIA
Brufani Palace (€€€)
Many of the rooms in this elegant hotel have beamed ceilings,
antique furniture and superb views of the city.
✉ Piazza Italia 12 ☎ 0755 32541; www.brufanipalace.com

PISA
Hotel Roma (€)
Simple, comfortable rooms close to the Campo dei Miracoli.
✉ Via Bonnano 111 ☎ 50 550 164; www.pisaonline.it/hotelroma

SIENA
Duomo (€€)

Well placed for Siena's main sights, with excellent views. Simply furnished rooms have safes and baths. Breakfast included.

✉ Via Stalloreggi 38 ☎ 0577 289 088; www.hotelduomo.it

SPOLETO
Hotel dei Duchi (€€)

Set amid trees and gardens on the edge of the historic centre, this modern hotel has well-furnished rooms and a terrace restaurant.

✉ Viale Matteotti 4 ☎ 0743 44541; www.hoteldeiduchi.it

URBINO
Bonconte (€€)

Peaceful townhouse hotel with antique furniture and comfortable bedrooms and bathrooms. Excellent breakfast buffet (included).

✉ Via delle Mura 28 ☎ 0722 2463

RESTAURANTS

ANCONA
La Moretta (€€)

This family-run restaurant in the old centre offers local specialities such as seafood pasta, crêpes and lamb.

✉ Piazza Plebiscito 52 ☎ 0712 02317 🕓 Lunch, dinner. Closed Sun

AREZZO
Antica Trattoria da Guido (€)

Serves home-made pasta, superb cuts of local meat and Arezzo specialities such as boned, stuffed rabbit and *taglioline*.

✉ Via Madonna del Prato 85 ☎ 0575 23760 🕓 Lunch, dinner. Closed period Aug and Dec

ASCOLI PICENO
C'era Una Volta (€)

Excellent views accompany the good, simple, traditional Marche food and wine; just outside Ascoli Piceno.

✉ Via Piagge 336, Piagge ☎ 0736 261 780 🕓 Lunch, dinner. Closed Tue

FLORENCE
Coco Lezzone (€€)
One of the last of Florence's truly traditional *trattorie*, serving freshly prepared local dishes in old-fashioned surroundings.

✉ Via Parioncino 26r ☎ 055 287 178 🕐 Lunch, dinner. Closed Sun and Tue pm, period in Aug and Christmas

Enoteca Pinchiorri (€€€)
One of Italy's most famous and prestigious restaurants where the quality of the food is matched by the superb wines and service.

✉ Via Ghibellina 87 ☎ 055 242 777 🕐 Lunch, dinner. Closed Sun, Mon and lunchtime Tue and Wed

ORVIETO
I Sette Consoli (€€)
You can eat in the garden in summer. Good *menù degustazione*.

✉ Piazza Sant'Angelo 1 ☎ 0763 343 911 🕐 Lunch, dinner. Closed Sun dinner (Nov–Mar), Wed and part of Feb

PISA
La Grotta (€€)
The menu and wine list change constantly. Particularly good meat *secondi*, *antipasti* and *primi*, and the desserts are also excellent.

✉ Via San Francesco 103 ☎ 050 578 105 Lunch, dinner. Closed Sun, Aug, Christmas–New Year

PISTOIA
Lo Storno (€)
This 600-year-old *osteria* offers simple, no-frills Tuscan cuisine.

✉ Via del Lastrone 8 ☎ 0573 21 693 🕐 Mon–Wed lunch only, Thu–Sat lunch, dinner. Closed Sun, Aug

SAN GIMIGNANO
Osteria delle Catene (€€)
Authentic, good-value establishment. The good local wine list features resinous Vernaccia di San Gimignano among the whites.

✉ Via Mainardi 18 ☎ 0577 941 966 🕐 Lunch, dinner. Closed Wed, Jan–Feb

SIENA

Marsili (€€€)

This elegant restaurant, in a vaulted medieval room, serves superb Sienese cooking, with many dishes based on ancient recipes.

✉ Via del Castoro 3 ☎ 0577 471 154 🕐 Lunch, dinner. Closed Mon

La Taverna del Capitano (€€)

You can choose from a range of Tuscan specialities at this family-run restaurant near the Duomo. Try the grilled pecorino cheese with radicchio or home-made pasta such as *pici* with garlic sauce.

✉ Via del Capitano 6–8 ☎ 0577 288 094 🕐 Lunch, dinner. Closed Tue and period in Nov

TODI

La Mulinella (€)

Just outside Todi, with good views from its garden, serving unpretentious local dishes.

✉ Ponte Naia 29 ☎ 075 894 4779 🕐 Lunch, dinner. Closed Wed, Nov

URBINO

Il Cortegiano (€€€)

Central Italian cuisine (including truffles); outdoor dining in summer.

✉ Via Puccinotti 13 ☎ 0722 320 307 🕐 Lunch, dinner. Closed Sun Nov–Mar

VOLTERRA

Trattoria del Sacco Fiorentino (€€)

Beyond the *trattoria*, which serves dishes based on regional specialities, is a wine bar offering delicious *primi* and *secondi*.

✉ Piazza XX Settembre 18 ☎ 0588 88 537 🕐 Lunch, dinner. Closed Wed and part of Jan and Feb

SHOPPING

CRAFTS, GIFTS AND SOUVENIRS

Farmacia di Santa Maria Novella

Old-world apothecary in Florence selling its own herbal elixirs, soaps and other concoctions, made from old monks' recipes.

✉ Via della Scala 16, Florence ☎ 055 216 276, 055 288 658

FASHION AND ACCESSORIES
Emilio Pucci
Florence's own designer is famous for his 1960s-style clothes.

✉ Via dei Tornabuoni 20–22r, Florence ☎ 055 265 8082

FOOD AND DRINK
Enoteca Provinciale
Wide selection of wines from Umbria and other Italian regions.

✉ Via Ulisse Rocchi 16–18, Perugia ☎ 075 572 4824

SHOES AND LEATHER
Salvatore Ferragamo
Makes some of the most sought-after shoes in the world.

✉ Via de' Tornabuoni 16, Florence ☎ 055 292 123

ENTERTAINMENT

NIGHTLIFE
Auditorium Flog
This is where the best and most famous jazz and rock musicians come to play in Florence. Open for concerts only.

✉ Via Mercati 24, Florence ☎ 055 490 437; www.flog.it

Jazz Club
Drinks and snacks accompany concerts or other musical events most evenings at this historic haunt of Florence's jazz *aficionados*.

✉ Via Nuova de' Caccini 3, Florence ☎ 055 247 9700

Rivoire
A beautiful marble interior and tables on Piazza Signoria make this a compulsory (if expensive) spot for an evening drink or aperitif.

✉ Piazza Signoria 5r, Florence ☎ 055 211 302

OPERA, BALLET AND THEATRE
Teatro Comunale
During the winter, the headquarters of Maggio Musicale Fiorentino is used for classical music concerts, opera and ballet.

✉ Corso Italia 16, Florence ☎ 055 27791; tickets 899 666 805

Southern Central Italy

Roma

This is the area in which the rich, cosmopolitan north meets the more traditional, mellow *mezzogiorno* (south) – not just geographically but culturally and gastronomically as well.

The best place to see the resulting blend of cut-and-thrust northern Europe with the slower paced Mediterranean way of life is Rome, where politicians and business people rush through sun-soaked piazzas and strolling crowds.

Apart from Rome and its immediate vicinity, south central Italy is slightly off the tourist track and even the beaches, while just as well developed as those elsewhere in Italy, don't attract the same international crowd, catering instead to hordes of weekenders from nearby towns and cities.

To the east of Rome lie the rugged mountains of Abruzzo and Molise. Here, age-old isolated communities serve as centres for hillwalking in summer and skiing in winter.

ROMA (ROME)

Italy's capital has almost 3,000 years of history packed into the narrow, winding streets and majestic *piazzas* of its historic centre. Its greatest monuments include the civic and religious head-quarters of an ancient empire, churches founded during the earliest days of Christianity, and pompous baroque palaces built for the powerful noble families who amassed vast collections of works by the great artists they patronized.

✚ 12J

ℹ️ Via Parigi 5 ☎ 06 488 991; www.romaturismo.it

Basilica di San Pietro and Il Vaticano

Best places to see, ➤ 36–37.

Bocca della Verità

In the portico of the 12th-century church of Santa Maria in Cosmedin (note the fine inlaid Cosmati marble pavement inside) is a strange, ancient marble face (originally a drain cover) with an open mouth. Legend has it that the mouth of truth will clamp shut on the hand of anybody who lies – during the Middle Ages it was a common test of wives' marital fidelity. Across the road are the rectangular temple of Portunus from the 2nd century BC and the round temple of Hercules from the 1st century BC.

✚ *Roma 5e* ✉️ Santa Maria in Cosmedin, Via Teatro di Marcello 🚌 81, 160, 715

Campidoglio

Michelangelo designed Rome's magnificent civic centre, which today houses the mayor's office in the Palazzo Senatorio and the **Musei Capitolini** in the flanking Palazzo Nuovo and Palazzo dei Conservatori. The central *piazza* contains a copy of the 2nd-century AD statue of Marcus Aurelius. Highlights of the main museum include the sensual *Dying Gaul*, the delightful 1st-century BC *Spinario* (a bronze of a boy extracting a thorn from his foot) and the *She-Wolf Suckling Romulus and Remus* (symbol of Rome). The original statue of Marcus Aurelius, still with traces of its old gilding, is displayed in the Exhedra on the first floor. The picture gallery contains works by Caravaggio and Tintoretto. In the late 1990s the museums underwent a major renovation and some of the priceless ancient statues were transferred to the incongruous yet atmospheric surroundings of a former electricity power plant near Ostiense station, the Central Montemartin.

➕ *Roma 6d*

Musei Capitolini

✉ Piazza del Campidoglio ☎ 06 8205 9127; www.museicapitolini.org ⏰ Tue–Sun 9–8
💰 Expensive 🚌 40, 60, 86, 88, 590, 715

Castel Sant'Angelo

Built by Emperor Hadrian (AD117–138) as a
mausoleum for himself, the *castel* was used as a
defensive stronghold by generations of popes from
the Middle Ages until the unification of Italy. Since
1886 it has been open to the public, who enter
via the original ramp used by Hadrian's funeral
procession. Other highlights include a courtyard with
Montelupo's statue of an angel (1544) sheathing a
sword, and a Michelangelo gateway (1514). Off the
courtyard are the delicately frescoed, 16th-century
state rooms including the Sala di Apollo, where
holes in the floor lead to notorious prisons, and the
magnificent Sala Paolina, with a delightfully enigmatic
trompe l'oeil door. There are good views over Rome
from the ramparts.

✚ *Roma 3C* ✉ Lungotevere Castello 50 ☎ 06 681 9111
🕐 Tue–Sun 9–7:30 💶 Expensive 🚌 23, 40, 64

Foro Romano, Palatino and Colosseo
Best places to see, ➤ 44–45.

Galleria Borghese

The sculpture, on the ground floor, includes important classical works (*Sleeping Hermaphrodite, Dancing Faun*) and Canova's famous sculpture of Napoleon's sister, Pauline Bonaparte Borghese, as a seductive Venus. The highlights, however, are the spectacular early sculptures by Bernini, showing his precocious talent in works such as *The Rape of Proserpine*. Among the celebrated paintings on the ground-floor walls and upstairs are a *Deposition* by Raphael; Titian's early masterpiece, *Sacred and Profane Love*; a rich, vibrant *Last Supper* by Jacopo Bassano; and Correggio's erotic *Danaë*. The six Caravaggio paintings include his important early work, the luscious *Boy with a Fruit Basket*.

➕ *Roma 7a* ✉ Piazzale del Museo Borghese 5 ☎ 06 841 6542 🕐 Tue–Sun 9–7 (advance booking compulsory) 💵 Expensive 🚌 52, 53, 88, 116, 119, 910

Palazzo Altemps

This lovingly restored baroque *palazzo* is the perfect setting for the vast ancient sculpture collection amassed in the 16th century by Prince Ludovisi. The prince hired some of the best sculptors of his own time (including Bernini and Algardi) to patch up damaged specimens among his newly acquired Greek and Roman masterpieces. Some of the results are ridiculous, with spare heads and limbs spliced on to unmatching torsos. However, even the most demanding ancient-art purists will delight in the Aldovisi Throne, a

serene 5th-century BC portrayal of the goddess Aphrodite.

➕ *Roma 4c* ✉ Piazza Sant'Apollinare 6 ☎ 06 3996 7700 🕐 Tue–Sun 9–7:45 💵 Moderate 🚌 70, 81, 87, 115, 116, 186, 492, 628

Palazzo Barberini

A national art gallery since 1949, this is one of Rome's grandest baroque palaces – Carlo Maderno, Bernini and Borromini all worked on its exterior, while its sumptuous interior includes an elaborate ceiling fresco by Pietro da Cortona in the *Gran Salone*. The collection gives a good overview of (principally Italian) 13th- to 17th-century painting but excels in its 16th- and 17th-century paintings by the likes of Andrea del Sarto, Raphael, Bernini, El Greco, Bronzino, Guido Reni, Guercino and Caravaggio.

✚ *Roma 7c* ✉ Via Quattro Fontane 13 ☎ 06 482 4184 🕐 Tue–Sun 8:30–7 ✋ Moderate 🚌 60, 61, 62, 175, 492, 590

Palazzo Doria Pamphilj

This has been the seat of the noble Roman family of Doria Pamphilj since the late Renaissance. In the grand reception rooms and picture galleries, with their elaborate frescoed ceilings, the paintings are hung exactly as they were in the 18th century, cluttered side by side from floor to ceiling. They include works by Memling, Raphael, Titian, Tintoretto and

Caravaggio. The star of the collection is Velásquez's portrait of Pope Innocent X.

www.doriapamphilj.it

✚ *Roma 5d* ✉ Piazza del Collegio Romano 2 ☎ 06 679 7323 🕐 Daily 10–5 ✋ Expensive

Palazzo Massimo alle Terme

This beautiful museum forms part of the Museo Nazionale Romano and its collections include works of art from the 2nd and 1st centuries BC to the 4th century AD, with some original Greek works from the 5th century BC. Among these are the superb *Niobid* (440BC), once the property of Julius Caesar, and the *Discobolus*, a bronze figure of a discus thrower. Look for the *Sleeping Hermaphrodite*, a Dionysian cult reclining figure of great eroticism, the wall paintings from the House of Livia (20–10BC) and the mosaic floor showing a hippopotamus hunt by the Nile.

✠ *Roma 8c* ✉ Largo di Villa Peretti 1 ☎ 06 396 7700 🕐 Tue–Sun 9–7:45 ✋ Moderate 🚌 61, 62, 84, 90, 92, 105 🚇 Repubblica/Termini

Pantheon

Erected by Marcus Agrippa (1st century AD), this awe-inspiring temple to all the gods became a Christian church in 609 and contains the tombs of Raphael and Vittorio Emanuele II, the first king of united Italy. It is a miracle of ancient engineering: the massive semicircular dome, 43.3m (142ft) in diameter, was constructed by pouring concrete over a wooden framework. The huge bronze doors are ancient Roman and the ornate marble floor is a 19th-century reconstruction of the original.

✠ *Roma 5d* ✉ Piazza della Rotonda ☎ 06 6830 0230 🕐 Mon–Sat 8:30–6 (7:30 in summer), Sun 9–6 ✋ Free 🚌 116 to Via della Palombella

Piazza Navona

One of the world's most beautiful squares owes its elongated shape to the 1st-century AD stadium over which it was built (remains lie to its north). The centrepiece is Bernini's *Fontana dei Fiumi* (1651), featuring symbolic representations of the rivers Ganges, Danube, Plate and Nile clinging to a massive artificial cliff-face, in front of the church of Sant'Agnese in Agone. The figure at the centre of the fountain to the southeast is by Bernini.

✠ *Roma 4c* 🚌 70, 81, 87, 115, 116, 186, 492, 628

a walk in Rome's historic centre

Combine this walk with visits to the Forum (➤ 44) and the Vatican (➤ 36–37) and you can claim to have seen the best of Rome.

From Largo Argentina head down Corso Vittorio Emanuele II and turn left (brown pedestrian sign) to the Campo de' Fiori, Rome's most atmospheric market square. From here, walk through Piazza della Cancelleria back to the Corso and cross the road diagonally right to Piazza San Pantaleo. Follow the brown signs to Piazza Navona (➤ 155). Exit the piazza right down Corso Agone; ahead is Palazzo Madama.

This 16th-century palace is now the seat of the Italian Senate.

Behind it, turn left down Via della Dogana Vecchia to the church of San Luigo dei Francesi, which has superb paintings by Caravaggio. Cross the road and follow the brown signs to the Pantheon (➤ 155). Facing the building, head left up Via del Semnario and through Piazza Sant'Ignazio to Via del Corso. Turn left, cross the Corso and follow the brown signs to the Fontana di Trevi.

This dramatic fountain was designed in 1762 by Nicola Salvi); throw a coin into it over your left shoulder if you want to return to Rome.

Turn left along Via Stamperia to Via del Tritone, where you cross and take Via Due Macelli, which leads to Piazza di Spagna and the famous Spanish Steps.

Pause on the Spanish Steps, designed by Francesco de Sanctis and built in the 1720s.

Climb the steps, turn left and walk past the Villa Medici and along the edge of the Pincio until you see Piazza Santa Maria del Popolo, with its Egyptian obelisk, below you.

Santa Maria del Popolo church contains the *Conversion of St Paul* and the *Crucifixion of St Peter* by Caravaggio.

Distance 4.5km (3 miles)
Time 1.5 hours without stops, 3–4 hours with stops
Start point Largo Argentina
✚ *Roma 5d*
End point Piazza del Popolo
✚ *Roma 5a*
🚇 Flaminio
Lunch Hostaria Romanesca (€)
✉ Campo de'Fiori 40

San Clemente

A tour of this three-layered building starts with a 12th-century church containing a contemporary apse mosaic, a 6th-century choir stall and Masolini frescoes of St Catherine of Alexandria. Beneath this is a 4th-century church containing 11th-century frescoes of St Clement and a large circular well, probably a font. Below this are ancient Roman remains, including a cramped Mithraeum (temple of Mithras) with a small altar with a relief of Mithras slaying a bull. The route back up passes through the walls of ancient Roman apartment blocks.

✚ *Roma 8e* ✉ Via San Giovanni in Laterano ☎ 06 7045 1018 🕔 Mon–Sat 9–12:30, 3–6, Sun 10–12:30, 3–6 ♿ Inexpensive; upper church free 🚌 85, 167, 850

San Giovanni in Laterano

This was the home of the papacy from the 4th to the 14th centuries, and is now the Cathedral of Rome (the pope doubles up as Bishop of Rome). The building is 16th century with a portico

(1585) by Fontana, facade by Galilei and nave (1650) by Borromini. Inside are remnants of earlier buildings, and 5th-century mosaics in the baptistery.

➕ *Roma 8e (off map)* ✉ Piazza San Giovanni in Laterano ☎ 06 6988 6568 🕐 Basilica: 7–7 (6 in winter); Baptistery: daily 7–12:30, 4–7:30; Cloisters: 9–6 (5 in winter) 🚌 30b, 81, 85, 87, 186, 590, 850

Santa Maria Maggiore

This hefty edifice has a ceiling clad in some of the first gold to be brought back from the New World. The Cappelle Sistina (1585) and Paolina (1611) contain important artworks, but the basilica's main glory lies in its mosaics. In the nave is a 5th-century narrative of the Old Testament and, in the apse, an impressive *Glorification of Mary* (1295). The site of the church is said to have been decided by the Virgin sending an unseasonal fall of snow to this spot, an event still commemorated every August.

➕ *Roma 8d* ✉ Piazza di Santa Maria Maggiore ☎ 06 483 195 🕐 Summer 7–7; winter 9–5 🚌 16, 70, 71, 75, 204, 590

Trastevere

Trastevere – across the Tiber – is a traditional working-class area, today renowned for its restaurants, cafés and quirky shops. It's a great place for serendipitous discoveries, though you shouldn't miss its main churches, Santa Maria in Trastevere and Santa Cecilia. The former, set on an attractive piazza, dates from the 12th century and has wonderful Byzantine frescoes in the apse and along the nave, while Santa Cecilia was built on the traditional site of the martyrdom of the patron saint of music.

➕ *Roma 3f* 🚌 23, 44, 280, 780

More to see in Southern Central Italy

CASTELLI ROMANI

The small medieval towns on the slopes of the Alban Hills are close enough to Rome to be reachable for lunch – or even dinner if you have a car. The white wines they produce are often served as *vino della casa* in Rome's restaurants and *trattorie*. Frascati, the nearest of the Castelli, is dominated by the **Villa Aldobrandini** (1598–1603), while Rocca di Papa is the highest (680m/2,230ft) and has fine medieval buildings; the main piazza of Ariccia is adorned by Bernini, and Albano Laziale has Etruscan and Roman ruins. The pope's summer residence is at **Castel Gandolfo.**

✚ 12J (Frascati and Castel Gandolfo)

🛈 APT Piazza Marconi 1, Frascati ☎ 06 942 0331

Villa Aldobrandini

✉ Piazzale Marconi, Frascati ☎ 06 942 0331 🕙 Mon–Fri 9–1, 3–6 (5 in winter)

Castel Gandolfo

✉ Piazza Plebiscito

ETRURIA

The region of Lazio settled by the Etruscans includes Tarquinia, 2km (1.2 miles) southeast of which are magnificent painted tombs in the Necropoli di Monterozzi. Tarquinia also has a well-stocked **Museo Nazionale.** Another major Etruscan centre is Cerveteri, where one of the highlights of the Necropoli di Banditaccia (2km/1.2 miles north) is the Tomb of the Reliefs, showing scenes from everyday Etruscan life. Vulci, Norchia and Tuscania also have Etruscan remains.

www.tarquinia.net

✚ 11J (Tarquinia and Cerveteri)

Museo Nazionale di Tarquinia

✉ Piazza Cavour ☎ 0766 856 036 🕙 Tue–Sun 8:30–7:30. Closed public hols 🖐 Expensive (includes visit to necropolis)

L'AQUILA

Gran Sasso (2,914m/9,557ft), the highest of the Apennines, towers above L'Aquila, the capital of Abruzzo, and can best be seen from the majestic 16th-century Castello, which now houses the **Museo Nazionale d'Abruzzo** with its fine collection of art from ancient to modern times. The symbolic Fontana delle 99 Cannelle (Fountain of the 99 Spouts, 1272, but much restored since) has a spout for each of the communities involved in the city's founding in 1240.

Other prime monuments are the churches of Santa Maria di Collemaggio (started in 1287), with its pink and white geometric facade (14th century), and San Bernardino (1454–72), whose 17th-century restoration includes a baroque ceiling.

www.abruzzoturismo.it;
www.parks.it

✚ 13J

Museo Nazionale d'Abruzzo

✉ Viale Benedetto Croce ☎ 0862 633 229 🕒 Tue–Sun 9–8. Closed public hols ♿ Moderate

OSTIA ANTICA

Although nothing like as complete as Pompei (➤ 50–51), this ancient Roman port (now a long way from the sea) has some fine remains dating from the 1st century BC to the 4th century AD. These stand in a pretty area of encroaching vegetation that creates a park-like atmosphere. Highlights include the mosaics of the Piazzale delle Corporazioni, representing the trading interests of the corporations whose offices stood here; the thermopolium, where hot food and drinks were served (note the illustrated, frescoed menu); the nearby Casa di Diana apartment block; the Terme di Nettuno baths; and a theatre.

www.ostiaantica.net

✚ 11J ✉ Via Romagnoli 717, Ostia Antica ☎ 06 5635 2830 🕓 Apr–Sep Tue–Sun 8:30–6; Oct–Mar Tue–Sun 8:30–4 ✋ Moderate 🚇 Metro from Rome to Magliana, then train to Ostia Antica

PARCO NAZIONALE D'ABRUZZO

These 40,000ha (98,840 acres) of mountain wilderness are covered with dense beech and maple forests and shelter many wild animals, including about 100 Marsican brown bears, Apennine wolves, golden eagles, Abruzzo chamois and wild cats. (If you don't spot these in the wild, you can go to the zoo near the park's headquarters to see convalescing injured animals.) The park is well laid out with marked trails, picnic areas and campsites.

www.parcoabruzzo.it; www.parks.it
🕂 13J ✉ Headquarters: Via Consultore 1, Pescasseroli ☎ 0863 91 955
🚌 Bus from Avezzano or Alfedena

TIVOLI

Most people come to this hillside town to see the spectacular terraced gardens of the **Villa d'Este** (1550), where the statuary, including a row of grotesque heads spitting water, outdoes the plant life. Nearby are the stately remains of the **Villa Adriana.** Built for Emperor Hadrian between AD118 and 134, this is a vast area of ruined follies, including a massive fishpond, the circular Teatro Marittimo on an island in an artificial lake, and many nymphaeums. There are also temples, barracks and a museum.

🕂 12J 🚌 Bus from Rome
ℹ️ APT Piazza Garibaldi, Tivoli ☎ 0774 311 249

Villa d'Este
✉ Piazza Trento, Tivoli ☎ 199 766 166 🕐 Tue–Sun 8:30 to one hour before sunset ✋ Expensive

Villa Adriana
☎ 0774 382 733 🕐 Mar–Oct daily 9–6; Nov–Feb daily 9–3:30 ✋ Expensive
🚃 Train from Rome to Tivoli, then No 4 bus to Villa Adriana

HOTELS

ABRUZZO NATIONAL PARK
Paradiso (€)
Unpretentious family hotel perfectly placed for the Parco
Nazionale. Good home cooking in the restaurant.
✉ Via Fonte Fracassi 4, Pescasseroli ☎ 0863 910 422; www.albergo-
paradiso.it 🕐 Closed most of Nov

CASTELLI ROMANI
Colonna (€)
This welcoming hotel in the heart of Frascati makes a good base
for the Castelli; expect comfortable bedrooms, a lavish breakfast
buffet and log fires in the lounge area in winter.
✉ Piazza del Gesù 12, Frascati ☎ 0694 018 088; www.hotelcolonna.it

ETRURIA
Al Gallo (€€)
Delightful little hotel in Tuscania's historic centre, with antiques
among its tasteful furnishings. Good breakfast included in the
price. The hotel's restaurant is one of the best in the area.
✉ Via del Gallo 22, Tuscania ☎ 0761 443 388; www.algallo.it

ROME
Campo dei Fiori (€€)
See page 75.

Hassler Villa Medici (€€€)
One of the grandest old-style luxury hotels in the city (above the
Spanish Steps). There's a view to die for from the stunning roof
terrace and restaurant.
✉ Piazza Trinità dei Monti 6 ☎ 06 699 340; www.hotelhasslerroma.com

Hotel Aberdeen (€)
There's good value for money and a wonderfully quiet atmosphere
at this friendly hotel just off the Via Nazionale. Most rooms are a
good size and a breakfast buffet is served in a frescoed room.
✉ Via Firenze 48 ☎ 06 482 3920

Hotel Antico Borgo di Trastevere (€)

This pretty hotel, in the heart of lively Trastevere with its great nightlife, has comfortable rooms with beamed ceilings and exposed brickwork, though some are quite small. It's a 15-minute walk to the historic centre across the river, and about the same to the Vatican.

✉ Vicolo del Buco ☎ 06 588 3774; www.trasteverehouse.it

RESTAURANTS

ABRUZZO NATIONAL PARK
Plistia (€€)

Abruzzese cuisine at its very best in this attractive, well-run restaurant attached to a hotel. *Menù degustazione* with eight courses.

✉ Via Principe di Napoli 28, Pescasseroli ☎ 0863 910 732 ⏱ Lunch, dinner. Closed Mon

CASTELLI ROMANI
Cacciani (€€€)

Dine on the terrace of this beautiful restaurant and enjoy dishes such as tender baby lamb, *saltimbocca alla romana* and mouthwatering desserts while you gaze out over the town.

✉ Via Armando Diaz 13, Frascati ☎ 0694 20378 ⏱ Lunch, dinner. Closed Mon, period in Jan and Aug

L'AQUILA
Trattoria del Giaguaro (€€)

Robust Abruzzese fare that includes *macaroni alla chitarra* and filling meat dishes.

✉ Piazza Santa Maria Paganica 1 ☎ 0862 28 249 ⏱ Lunch, dinner. Closed Mon dinner, Tue, two weeks in Jul and Aug, Christmas

OSTIA ANTICA
Il Monumento (€€)

Simple, well-made fish dishes at this *trattoria* in the village near the excavations. *Spaghetti monumento* contains a mix of seafood.

✉ Piazza Umberto I 18 ☎ 06 565 0021 ⏱ Lunch, dinner. Closed Mon

ROME
Il Convivio (€€€)
Creative cuisine served with a touch of genius; good set menus and extensive wine list for special occasions.

✉ Via dei Soldati 31 ☎ 06 686 9432 🕐 Lunch, dinner. Closed Sun, Aug

Dal Cavalier Gino (€€)
This traditional restaurant next door to the Parliament building has a daily menu of specials featuring home-made pasta and desserts.

✉ Vicolo Rosini 4 ☎ 06 687 434 🕐 Lunch, dinner. Closed Sun and Aug

Pizzeria San Calisto (€)
Vast, thin-crust pizzas topped with tasty, fresh ingredients in the bustling Trastevere district. Outdoor eating in summer.

✉ Piazza San Calisto 9 ☎ 06 581 8256 🕐 Lunch, dinner. Closed Mon

SHOPPING

CRAFTS, GIFTS AND SOUVENIRS
Spazio Sette
Not cheap, but the best homeware shop in central Rome, selling everything from glassware to hardware, postcards to furniture.

✉ Via dei Barbieri 7, Rome ☎ 06 6880 4261

FASHION AND ACCESSORIES
Gucci
Mouthwatering classics at this chic Italian designer's outlet.

✉ Via Condotti 8, Rome ☎ 06 678 9340

Marini
Big designer names in lingerie, nightwear and swimwear.

✉ Via Sicilia 32, Rome ☎ 06 488 5315

Valentino
Rome's own designer has his boutique in Via Condotti, just two doors from the wonderful headquarters in Piazza Mignatelli. The casual wear outlet, Oliver, is around the corner on Via del Babuino.

✉ Via Condotti, Rome ☎ 06 678 5862

FOOD AND DRINK
Ai Monasteri
Seven monasteries send their produce for sale to this shop. Honey, liqueurs, preserves, natural toiletries and skin products.
✉ Corso Rinascimento 72, Rome ☎ 06 6880 2783

MARKETS
Porta Portese
Rome's famous flea market takes over the streets near Trastevere every Sunday morning. You can buy almost anything imaginable, from clothes (beware of fake labels) to books and antiques.
✉ Via Porta Portese, Rome

ENTERTAINMENT

NIGHTLIFE
Alexanderplatz
Rome's flagship jazz club; the best the capital has to offer.
✉ Via Ostia 9, Roma ☎ 06 3974 2171; www.alexanderplatz.it

Alpheus
Three separate areas: one for jazz, one for rock and the other for a disco.
✉ Via del Commercio 36, Roma ☎ 06 574 7826; www.alpheus.it

Big Mama
Sub-titled 'the home of the blues in Rome', Big Mama has an interesting programme of live music performed by Italian and international musicians, including the occasional legend.
✉ Vicolo San Francesco a Ripa 18, Rome ☎ 06 581 2551; www.bigmama.it

The Gallery
This streamlined, energy-filled bar-cum-club behind the Pantheon pulls in the crowds with its mix of R&B, hip-hop and hits from the '70s and '80s.
✉ Via della Maddalena 12, Rome ☎ 06 687 2316; www.thegallery.it

Gilda

The establishment place to dance (or watch others), frequented by politicians and TV personalities, among others.

✉ Via Mario de' Fiori 97, Rome ☎ 06 678 4838

Goa

Bright, lively nightclub with a weekly gay night and lots of house, jungle, tech house and other types of music.

✉ Via Libetta 13, Rome ☎ 06 574 8277

OPERA, BALLET AND THEATRE

Associazione di Santa Cecilia

The Accademia has among Rome's best chamber and symphony orchestras. Performances take place in the Parco della Musica, the city's new auditorium.

✉ Viale Pietro de Coubertin 34, Rome ☎ 06 808 2058 (ticket office); www.santacecilia.it

Teatro Agorà

This theatre hosts visiting theatre companies from the rest of Europe, who perform plays in their native tongue.

✉ Via della Penitenza 33, Roma ☎ 06 687 4167

Teatro Argentina

One of the homes of the Italian National Theatre, which stages good, traditional performances of classic plays. In summer they move to the Roman theatre at Ostia Antica (➤ 162).

✉ Largo di Torre Argentina 52, Roma ☎ 06 6880 4601; www.teatrodiroma.net

SPORT

SOCCER

Anybody with any interest in soccer at all should try to attend a match when Roma or Lazio play (buy tickets in advance).

✉ Stadio Olimpico, Viale dello Stadio Olimpíco, Rome ☎ 06 323 7333; www.asroma.it (Roma); www.sslazio.it (Lazio)

Southern Italy, Sardinia and Sicily

The summer sun rules supreme in the *mezzogiorno* (the south), giving everything an added intensity: colours are brighter, sounds are louder, and flavours richer and more pungent. With the exception of Naples, the Costiera Amalfitana and parts of Sardinia and Sicily, this region is off the international tourist track, so there is plenty to discover.

Sardegna

Napoli

Sicilia

The landscape varies from hostile mountains in Basilicata to flat, fertile plains in Puglia and dramatic photogenic coasts in Campania and Calabria. In addition, both the mainland and the islands of Sardinia and Sicily are full of reminders of a long history and centuries of foreign occupation from all corners of Europe and the Mediterranean.

South Italy is dotted with prehistoric, Greek and Roman ruins,

Norman, Byzantine and Romanesque cathedrals, and effervescent baroque *palazzi* of a lighter, less pompous style than that of their contemporaries to the north.

NAPOLI (NAPLES)

You either love Naples or hate it; no visitor remains indifferent. This chaotic city, and its exuberant inhabitants, living on the coast beneath Vesuvius, have a character all of their own. In the 18th and 19th centuries, Naples was one of the main stops on the Grand Tour, but during the 20th century crumbling architecture and a soaring crime rate sent the city into decline. A major clean-up has greatly improved the situation, but it's still worth taking particular care of your valuables here.

✚ 14L

ℹ Via San Carlo 9 ☎ 081 402 394; Piazza del Gesù ☎ 081 551 2701; www.inaples.it

Castel Nuovo and Palazzo Reale

This pleasing caricature of a castle, with crenellations and stolid chess-piece towers, was rebuilt in the 15th century over a 12th-century original. Its majestic entrance is based on ancient Roman triumphal arches. Inside is the 14th-century Cappella Palatina (from the previous building), the

Museo Civico and 14th- to 18th-century art. The nearby **Palazzo Reale** was the Bourbon royal residence from 1734 to 1860. It contains antique furniture, a library of historic manuscripts, and Neapolitan frescoes (17th–18th centuries).

Castel Nuovo

✉ Piazza Municipio ☎ 081 795 5877 🕐 Mon–Sat 9–7 🖐 Moderate

Palazzo Reale

✉ Piazza Plebiscito ☎ 081 580 811 🕐 Thu–Tue 9–9. Closed early Mar, public hols 🖐 Moderate

Certosa di San Martino and Castel Sant'Elmo

On a hill with fine views over Naples' historic centre and the bay, this gem of Neapolitan baroque has aristocratic cloisters by Cosimo Fanzago, an opulent, marble-inlaid church and a fascinating museum of

traditional Christmas cribs, maps, art, and artefacts illustrating the history of Naples. Behind it stands the star-shaped Castel Sant'Elmo (14th century, rebuilt in the 16th), used as a prison in the 18th century and during the Risorgimento (19th century).

✉ Largo di San Martino 1 ☎ 081 578 4120

🕐 Mon–Sat 9–2 🖐 Inexpensive

Museo Archeologico Nazionale

If nothing else brings you to Naples, come for this stupendous mass of ancient Greek and Roman artefacts, one of the best such collections in the world. Among treasures too numerous to list are the largest surviving ancient group sculpture (*Amphion and Zethus Tying Dirce to the Horns of the Bull*, 200BC, from the extensive Farnese collection); some of the most beautiful frescoes, mosaics and other artworks from Pompei (➤ 50–51) and Herculaneum (➤ 177); portrait busts of great Greeks and Romans; and rooms dedicated to erotic art.

✉ Piazza Museo 19 ☎ 081 440 166 🕐 Wed–Mon 9–8 ✋ Expensive

Museo di Capodimonte

Naples' most important art gallery is housed in an 18th-century royal hunting lodge. This is one of the best collections in Italy, with Renaissance and baroque masterpieces (by Masaccio, Bernini, Correggio, Titian, Pieter Brueghel and others), and an interesting section with 19th-century Neapolitan painting.

✉ Via di Miano 1, Parco di Capodimonte ☎ 081 749 9111 🕓 Tue–Sun 8:30–7:30 ✋ Expensive

Quartieri Spagnoli

This grid of narrow streets below the Certosa di San Martino (➤ 171) was laid out by Spanish troops in the 17th century and is now a busy, inner-city residential area full of the sounds of people going about their day, and airing laundry – quintessential Naples, as seen in the movies.

✉ West of Via Toledo

San Lorenzo Maggiore and San Gregorio Armeno

Behind an 18th-century baroque facade lies the cool, simple Gothic interior of **San Lorenzo Maggiore** (14th century), whose tall, slender apse leads the eye automatically upwards. The Gothic mosaic-decorated tomb of Catherine of Austria (died 1323) is here. **San Gregorio Armeno,** around the corner, is a different story with its over-the-top baroque voluptuousness, which includes frescoes by Luca Giordano. The Benedictine convent attached to the church was a favourite among those daughters of the Neapolitan aristocracy who wished (or were forced) to take the veil.

San Lorenzo Maggiore
✉ Via Tribunali 316
San Gregorio Armeno
✉ Via San Gregorio Armeno 1

More to see in Southern Italy, Sardinia and Sicily

ALBEROBELLO

This beguiling little town makes the most of its role as the capital of *trulli* country. *Trulli* are the small white buildings with uncemented grey, conical stone roofs that have punctuated the landscape of central Puglia for centuries (although most of the ones you see today are at most 200 years old). As well as its streets of *trulli* (many of whose owners are only too happy to give you a guided tour), Alberobello boasts the *trullo* church of Sant'Antonio and the **Trullo Sovrano,** a museum devoted to the *trulli*.

➕ 19P

Trullo Sovrano

✉ Piazza Sacramento ☎ 080 432 6030; www.trullosovrano.org 🕐 Apr–Oct daily 10–6

✋ Inexpensive

BARI

The capital of Puglia has a labyrinthine historic centre in which the most impressive sights are the imposing **Castello** (1233), whose interesting interior contains casts of other Pugliese monuments, and the Basilica di San Nicola (1087), the first Norman church in the region and much copied elsewhere. The basilica's treasures include a fine 11th-century bishop's throne. One of the buildings based on San Nicola was Bari's

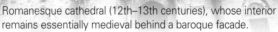

Romanesque cathedral (12th–13th centuries), whose interior remains essentially medieval behind a baroque facade.

✚ 18P

ℹ APT Piazza Moro 33a ☎ 080 524 2361

Castello

✉ Piazza Federico II di Svevia ☎ 080 528 6111 ⏰ Tue–Sun 8:30–7

👆 Inexpensive

BRINDISI

An important port since Roman times, this slightly drab city today swarms with backpackers and tourists on their way to the many Greece-bound ferries. The Roman column near the port marked the end of Via Appia, which has its beginning in Rome. Brindisi is not the most beautiful city in Italy, but its historic centre does have a certain run-down charm, and there are some good ancient vases in the **Museo Archeologico** opposite the Duomo.

✚ 20P

ℹ APT Lungomare Regina Margherita ☎ 0831 523 072

Museo Archeologico

✉ Piazza del Duomo 8 ☎ 0831 565 501 ⏰ Tue, Thu, Sat 9–1, 3:30–6:30, Wed, Fri Sun 9–1 👆 Free

CAPRI

During the day, this beautiful island turns into an anthill of activity as daytrippers are shunted around in a continuous stream of minibuses taking in sights that include the sculpted Faraglioni rocks off the northeast coast, the soothing Certosa di San Giacomo (14th century) in Capri town, and the cable-car from Anacapri to the island's highest point. The highlight, however, is the famous **Grotta Azzurra** (Blue Grotto) where little boats, packed like sardine tins, whoosh through a low opening into the extraordinary sea-filled hollow in the cliff-face.

www.capritourism.com

✚ 14L 🚢 Ferry from Naples, boats from Sorrento and other towns on the Costiera Amalfitana (➤ 40–41)

🛈 APT Piazza Umberto I ☎ 081 837 0686

Grotta Azzurra

🚢 Boat from Marina Grande in Capri harbour (not in rough weather)

✋ Expensive

CASTEL DEL MONTE

From the outside, this octagonal building with a tower on each of its corners resembles a massive sculpture. It was commissioned

by Emperor Frederick II in 1240 and is the most compelling and elaborate of the 200 fortresses he had built on his return from the Crusades. Inside, some of its plain, serene vaulted rooms are lined with marble, and there are wonderful views from the ramparts.

www.proloco.andria.ba.it

🏠 18P 🖂 Località Andria, Bari ☎ 0883 592 283 ⏰ Mar–Sep daily 10:15–7:45; Oct–Feb daily 9:15–6:45 ✋ Inexpensive

COSTIERA AMALFITANA

Best places to see, ➤ 40–41.

COSTIERA CALABRESE (CALABRIAN COAST)

The coast of Calabria has some of the cleanest water and most enticing beaches in Italy. Towns such as Scilla, Tropea, Maratea, Palmi and Pizzo are good centres from which to enjoy these, although a car is useful if you want to reach the quietest ones.

🏠 17R

ERCOLANO (HERCULANEUM)

The ancient city of Herculaneum (founded by the ancient Greeks) was buried by mud during the same eruption of Vesuvius that killed off Pompei (➤ 50–51). The excavations, while not as extensive as Pompei's, include some fine houses with mosaics, baths and a theatre.

🏠 14L 🖂 Corso Resina, Ercolano ☎ 081 777 7008; www.pompeiisites.org ⏰ Apr–Oct daily 8:30–7:30; Nov–Mar daily 8:30–5 ✋ Expensive

GARGANO

To the northeast of Foggia is the beautiful Gargano promontory, 10,000ha (24,700 acres) of which is covered with the dense beech, pine and maple trees of the Foresta Umbra. White beaches and bays of turquoise water line its coast. The most scenic stretch of road is the one between Mattinata and the resort of Vieste, which has a 13th-century cathedral and from where boats leave to the equally undeveloped Isole Tremiti.

✚ 15K 🚌 Bus to Manfredonia, Vieste, Mattinata, Peschici and Rodi

LECCE

Founded by the Romans, and still retaining its 1st century amphitheatre, Lecce today is renowned as southern Italy's most perfect baroque city. Late Renaissance prosperity funded the building of churches and *palazzi*, constructed from the local sandstone. This was carved into elaborate decorative facades of intricate fruit, garlands and flowers, far lighter in design and spirit than northern baqoque. Santa Croce, the Duomo, the Rosario and the Palazzo del Governo are the finest examples.

✚ 20Q

ℹ Via Vitorrio Emanuele 24 ☎ 0832 332 463; www.pugliaturismo.it

MATERA

A handsome Puglian-Romanesque 13th-century **Duomo** stands at the top of this Basilicata city, but it is the strange lower town, the *sassi* district, that is most fascinating. This consists of buildings, including churches and a few *palazzi*, scooped out of the rock and closed off with normal facades. The cave-dwelling habit was probably started by 8th-century monks and continued well into the 20th century, although by then many *sassi* had become uninhabitable and their occupants were rehoused. Major restorations are under way to revive this eerie ghost town.

➕ 18P

Duomo

✉ Piazza del Duomo

PAESTUM

The 6th-century BC Greek city of Poseidonia was taken over by the Romans in 273BC and continued to be occupied until malaria and the threat of Saracen attack led to its abandonment in the 9th century AD. Excavations, started in the 18th century, are among the most important in Italy. They include the temples of Neptune (5th century BC), Hera and Ceres (both 6th century BC), a stretch of city wall and a Roman forum. The museum has fine bas-reliefs among the other art and artefacts found on the site.

➕ 14L ✉ Via Magna Grecia, Zona Archeologica, Paestum ☎ 0828 811 016; www.infopaestum.it 🕐 Daily 9 to one hour before sunset. Museum: 9–7. Closed 1st and 3rd Mon of month, public hols ✋ Moderate

POMPEI

Best places to see, ➤ 50–51.

REGGIO DI CALABRIA

The main reason for venturing as far as this modern city in the toe of Italy (essentially rebuilt after an earthquake in 1908) is the **Museo Nazionale,** whose prime exhibits are two 5th-century BC Greek bronze statues of warriors, fished out of the sea in 1972. Highlights of the upstairs gallery include two 15th-century panel paintings by Antonello da Messina.

www.provincia.reggio-calabria.it

✚ 17T

Museo Nazionale

✉ Piazza de Nava 26 ☎ 0965 812 255 🕓 Daily 9–7:30. Closed 1st and 3rd Mon of month, public hols 🚼 Moderate

SARDEGNA (SARDINIA)

Sardinia's Costa Smeralda (Emerald Coast) has some of the most fashionable beach resorts in Europe, but, if you avoid the glitzy jetset Porto Cervo, you don't have to be a millionaire to enjoy the limpid, turquoise waters that lap this fascinating island's shores. Among its many natural wonders are caves (especially the Grotta di Nettuno), the rugged islands of the Arcipelago della Maddalena, the barren, wild Monti del Gennargentu, and the road between Arbatax and Dorgali.

Sardinia also has some of the oldest monuments in Europe: the unique *nuraghi* are conical buildings – of uncertain use – made out of blocks of stone and dating back as far as 1500BC. The best places to see *nuraghi* are Dorgali and Barumini. The island of Sant'Antioco has remains of the Phoenician and Roman settlement of Sulcis, and there are more Phoenician traces at Tharros. Remains from prehistoric and ancient Sardinia are in the

Museo Nazionale Archeologico in Cagliari, the enlarged island capital. The cathedral here has splendid 12th-century pulpits, carved by Guglielmo of Pisa with illustrations from the life of Christ. Sassari has the Museo Nazionale Sanna, another fine archaeological collection.

www.regione.sardegna.it

🚩 *Sardegna 2c* (Cagliari) 🛳 Ferry from mainland to Cagliari, Olbia and Porto Torres 🛫 Airports at Cagliari, Olbia and Alghero

Museo Nazionale Archeologico

✉ Cittadella dei Musei, Piazza Arsenale, Cagliari ☎ 070 684 000

🕐 Tue–Sun 9–8 ✋ Moderate

SICILIA (SICILY)

With a history during which Greek, Phoenician, Roman, Tunisian, Norman, French and Spanish occupations have all left their mark, Sicily has a culture and atmosphere that are subtly different from those of *il continente*, as mainland Italy is called here.

The vibrant city of **Palermo** is the capital. Its historic centre of crumbling baroque *palazzi* contains the Palazzo dei Normanni (Palace of the Normans) and the Cappella Palatina (Palatine Chapel), both with extraordinary Arab-Norman mosaics (12th century); the cathedral (12th to early 19th centuries); and the magnificent churches of La Martorana (Byzantine mosaics), San Giovanni degli Eremiti (Arab influenced) and San Cataldo (12th century). The Galleria Regionale della Sicilia has a major collection of Sicilian art, and the macabre Catacombe dei Cappuccini (Catacombs of the Capuchins) displays the clothed, mummified remains of 17th- to 19th-century Palermitani.

Near Palermo, the magnificently positioned Duomo at Monreale contains some of the most spectacular 12th- to 13th-century mosaics in existence. Segesta, to the west, has a splendid 5th-century BC temple and a 3rd-century BC theatre. East of Palermo, the pretty fishing village of Cefalù has a Norman cathedral (1131–1240), with more mosaics, and southeast of here, in the middle of Sicily, is Piazza Armerina, where well-preserved mosaics in the Roman villa (3rd–4th century AD) include representations of scantily clad female athletes. **Siracusa** (Syracuse) has a spectacular archaeological area, spanning many centuries of the town's development, a medieval-baroque centre and the Museo Archeologico Regionale. **Taormina**, in a beautiful setting with views of Mount Etna, has another ancient Greek theatre. See also Valle dei Templi (➤ 54–55).

www.palermotourism.com; www.insicilia.it

🗺 *Sicilia 2d* (Palermo) ⛴ Ferry from Naples or Genoa to Palermo or from Reggio di Calabria to Messina ✈ International flights to Palermo or Catania

ℹ Palermo: Piazza Castelnuovo 35 (☎ 091 605 8111). Piazza Armerina: Via Cavour 1 (☎ 0935 680 201). Siracusa: Via S Sebastiano 43 and 47 (☎ 0931 481 200). Taormina: Palazzo Corvaja, Corso Umberto I (☎ 0942 23 243)

HOTELS

ALBEROBELLO
Dei Trulli (€€€)
See page 74.

AMALFI COAST
Giordano (€€)
Simple, comfortable bedrooms and a friendly atmosphere in this little hotel surrounded by lovely grounds. Swimming pool.
✉ Via Santa Trinità 14, Ravello ☎ 089 857 170 🕐 Closed Jan–Feb

NAPLES
Vesuvio (€€€)
See page 74.

SARDINIA
Leonardo da Vinci (€€€)
In a central position near Sassari's archaeological museum. Spacious, modern bedrooms; suitable for families.
✉ Via Roma 79, Sassari ☎ 079 280 744; www.leonardodavincihotel.it

SICILY
Grand Hotel (€€€)
This art deco hotel, overlooking Porto Grande, offers a high level of comfort, a rooftop restaurant and some rooms with sea views.
✉ Viale Mazzini 12, Siracusa ☎ 0931 464 600; www.grandhotelsr.it

RESTAURANTS

ALBEROBELLO
La Cantina (€)
Friendly, family-run *trattoria* with a menu that changes seasonally.
✉ Vicolo F Lippolis 9 ☎ 080 432 3473 🕐 Lunch, dinner. Closed Tue (not in Aug), late Jun to mid-Jul

BARI
Terranima (€€)
The menu is seasonal and traditional and changes every 15 days.

✉ Via Putignani 213–215 ☎ 0805 219 725 🕐 Lunch, dinner. Closed Sun pm and Aug

CAPRI
La Rondinella (€€)
A delicious range of mainly fish-based *primi* and *secondi*.
✉ Via G Orlandi 295, Anacapri ☎ 081 837 1223 🕐 Lunch, dinner. Closed Thu and mid-Jan to mid-Feb

MATERA
Le Botteghe (€€)
Eat local and seasonal dishes in the heart of the *sassi* district.
✉ Piazza San Pietro Barisano 22 ☎ 0835 344 072 🕐 Lunch, dinner. Closed in Jan

NAPLES
La Chiacchierata (€€)
Authentic Neapolitan cuisine and atmosphere.
✉ Piazza Matilde Serao 37 ☎ 081 411 465 🕐 Lunch and Fri dinner (reserve for Friday evening). Closed Sun, Aug

PAESTUM
La Pergola (€€)
Delicious *antipasti* followed by fish, cheese and vegetable *primi*.
✉ Via Magna Grecia 1 ☎ 0828 723 377 🕐 Lunch, dinner. Closed Mon in winter

SARDINIA
Liberty (€€)
Sardinian fish dishes in a pretty art nouveau-style restaurant.
✉ Piazza N Sauro 3, Sassari ☎ 0792 36361 🕐 Lunch, dinner. Closed Sun May–Sep and 2 weeks in Aug

SICILY
Al Covo dei Beati Paoli (€€)
Sit inside or out and sample the seafood or fish, or one of the superb meat or vegetable dishes.

✉ Piazza Marina 50, Palermo ☎ 091 616 6634 🕐 Lunch, dinner.
Closed Mon

Archimede (€€)
Sicilian specialities include spaghetti in squid ink or with salty sea
urchins, followed by freshly caught fish and seafood.
✉ Via Gemmellaro 8, Siracusa ☎ 0931 69 701 🕐 Lunch, dinner; closed
Sun in winter

SHOPPING
CRAFTS, GIFTS AND SOUVENIRS
Associazione Figle d'Arte Cuticchio
Workshop which makes traditional Sicilian puppets used in the
attached puppet theatre. Takes special orders.
✉ Via Bara all'Olivella 95, Palermo ☎ 091 323 400

De Simone
Vibrant-coloured Sicilian ceramics painted with Palermitano motifs
and designs. Not the cheapest around but excellent quality.
✉ Piazza dei Leoni 2, Palermo ☎ 091 363 191

ENTERTAINMENT
NIGHTLIFE
Dreamer
The music ranges from rock via hip-hop and house to soul.
✉ Via Francesco de Sanctis, Naples ☎ 081 623 7769

Gambrinus
Sit outside at Naples' most famous café with its pleasant
atmosphere of faded splendour.
✉ Via Chiaia 1, Naples ☎ 081 417 582

Sottovento
The club where all the glitterati hang out on the Costa Smeralda.
✉ Porto Cervo, Arzachena ☎ 078 992 443

Sight Locator Index

This index relates to the maps on the covers. We have given map references to the main sights of interest in the book. Grid references in italics indicate sights featured on the Rome town plan. Some sights within towns may not be plotted on the maps.

Index

Acknowledgements

The Automobile Association wishes to thank the following photographers, companies and picture libraries for their assistance in the preparation of this book. Abbreviations for the picture credits are as follows – (t) top; (b) bottom; (l) left; (r) right; (c) centre; (AA) AA World Travel Library.

4l San Gimignano, AA/S McBride; **4c** Accademia Bridge, Venice, AA/A Mockford & N Bonetti; **4r** Colosseum, Rome, AA/A Kouprianoff; **5l** Grand Canal, Venice, AA/S McBride; **5c** Market, Cagliari, AA/C Sawyer; **6/7** San Gimignano, AA/S McBride; **8/9** Badia Fiorentian, Florence, AA/C Sawyer; **10/11t** Castelnuovo de Garfagnana, AA/K Paterson; **10/11b** Grand Canal, AA/C Sawyer; **10c** Fontana di Trevi, AA/S McBride; **10bl** Gardesana Occidentale, AA/A Mockford & N Bonetti; **10br** Sunflower, AA/K Paterson; **11c** Violin Maker, AA/C Sawyer; **12/13** Esquilino Market, Rome, AA/C Sawyer; **12** Pasta dishes, AA/E Meacher; **13c** Arezzo, AA/T Harris; **13b** Treviso market, AA/C Sawyer; **14t** Bakery, AA/C Sawyer; **14c** Vineyard, AA/K Paterson; **14b** Waiter, AA/C Sawyer; **14/15** Piazza Santa Maria della Pace, AA/A Kouprianoff; **15** Carrier bags, AA/C Sawyer; **16/17** Last Supper by Tintorertto, S. Trovaso, AA/A Mockford & N Bonetti; **16** Piazzo Campidoglio, AA/P Wilson; **17t** Cefalu Beach, AA/C Sawyer; **17b** Piazza della Signoria, ceremony, AA/S McBride; **18t** Ice-cream, Rome, AA/A Kouprianoff; **18c** Ice-cream, AA/C Sawyer; **18b** Cortona, AA/C Sawyer; **19** Monte Isola, AA/M Jourdan; **20/21** Accademia Bridge, AA/A Mockford & N Bonetti; **24** Calcio, Florence, AA/S McBride; **25** Carnival Mask, AA/D Miterdiri; **26** Marco Polo Airport, AA/C Sawyer; **28/29** Bus, AA/T Harris; **30/31** Telephone box, AA/T Harris; **34/35** Colosseum, AA/A Kouprianoff; **36** Sistine Chapel, AA/S McBride; **36/37** St Peter's Basilica, AA/A Kouprianoff; **37t** Piazza San Pietro, AA/D Miterdiri; **37b** Vatican Museum sign, AA/S McBride; **38/39** Accademia Bridge, AA/A Mockford & N Bonetti; **39** Grand Canal, AA/C Sawyer; **40** Villa Rufolo, Ravello, AA/M Jourdan; **40/41** Sorrento, AA/C Sawyer; **42/43** Duomo, Milan, AA/C Sawyer; **42 & 43** Duomo, Milan, AA/M Jourdan; **44/45t** Colosseum, AA/S McBride; **44/45b** Forum, AA/A Kouprianoff; **46** Uffizi Gallery, AA; **46/47** Uffizi Gallery, AA/C Sawyer; **47** Uffizi Gallery, AA/S McBride; **48t & 48b** Piazza San Marco, AA/A Mockford & N Bonetti; **49** Basilica San Marco, AA/S McBride; **50** Casa del Fauno, AA/M Jourdan; **50/51** Ruins at Pompei, AA/M Jourdan; **51** Vesuvius, AA/T Souter; **52, 52/53** Musoleo di Galla Placidia, AA/T Souter; **53** Basilica de S Vitale, AA/T Souter; **54/55 & 55** Valle dei Templi, AA/C Sawyer; **56/57** Grand Canal, AA/S McBride; **58/59** Osteria da Rioba, Grand Canal, Venice, AA/A Mockford & N Bonetti; **60** Fontana dei Fiumi, Rome, AA/C Sawyer; **62/63** View from Campanile, Venice, AA/A Mockford & N Bonetti; **64/65** Costa Smeralda, Sardinia, AA/C Sawyer; **65** Church of San Fransisco, Arezzo, AA/C Sawyer; **66/67** Campo Santa Margherita, AA/S McBride; **67** Moon engraving, AA/C Sawyer; **69** Giardini Pubblici, Milan, AA/M Jourdan; **70** Siena, clothes shop, AA/T Harris; **71** Mask shop, Venice, AA/A Mockford & N Bonetti; **72/73** Ca'Rezzonico, Venice AA/A Mockford & N Bonetti; **75** Gritti Palace Hotel, Venice, AA/A Mockford & N Bonetti; **76/77** Market, Cagliari, AA/C Sawyer; **79** Flowers, Vernazza, AA/T Souter; **80** Castello Sforzesco, Milan, AA/P Bennett; **80/81** Castello Sforzesco, Milan, AA/M Jourdan; **82/83** Galleria Vittorio Emanuele, Milan, AA/C Saywer; **83** Santa Maria Grazie, Milan, AA/M Jourdan; **84/85** Castello di Sarre, AA/C Sawyer; **85** Stradivarius statue, Cremona, AA/A Mockford & N Bonetti; **86/87** Cannero Riviera, AA/A Mockford & N Bonetti; **87** Isola Bella taxi boat, Stresa, AA/A Mockford; **88/89t** Bellagio, AA/M Jourdan; **88/89b** Torno, Lago di Como, AA/A Mockford & N Bonetti; **90/91** Portovenere, AA/T Souter; **92** Villa Reale di Stupinigi, Turin, AA/T Souter; **99** Duomo, Treviso, AA/C Sawyer; **100/101** Grand Canal, AA/S McBride; **101t** Galleria Accademia, Venice, AA/A Mockford & N Bonetti; **101b** Ca' d'Oro, Venice, AA/C Sawyer; **102** View from Campanile, Venice, AA/S McBride; **102/103** Santi Giovannie e Paolo, Venice, AA/S McBride; **103** Scuola di San Rocco, Crucifixion by Tintoretto, AA/D Miterdiri; **104/105** San Giorgio Maggiore, AA/S McBride; **106/107** Fontana del Nettuno, Bologna, AA/C Sawyer; **107** Arca di S Domenico, Bologna, AA/C Sawyer; **108/109** Ferrara, AA/C Sawyer; **110** Piazza Cermenati, Lecco, AA/M Jourdan; **111** Baptistery, Palma, AA/T Souter; **113** Piazza dei Signori, Treviso, AA/C Sawyer; **114/115** Arena, Verona, AA/T Souter; **121** Arezzo, AA/K Paterson; **122/123** Duomo, Florence, AA/K Paterson; **123** Galleria dell'Accademia, 'David', AA/S McBride; **124** Museo Nazionale del Bargello, AA/S McBride; **124/125** Palazzo Medici-Riccardi, AA/C Sawyer; **125** Palazzo Pitti, AA/S McBride; **126/127t** Ponte Vecchio, AA/S McBride; **126/127b** San Lorenzo Church, AA/T Harris; **127** San Marco Church, AA/S McBride; **128** Basilica di S Croce, AA/C Sawyer; **128/129** Santa Maria del Carmine, AA/C Sawyer; **129** Santa Maria Novella, AA/T Harris; **130** Market, Arezzo, AA/T Harris; **132/133c** Assisi, AA/K Paterson; **132/133b** Assisi, AA/P Davies; **133** Madonna del Calcinaio, AA/C Sawyer; **134** Portoferraio, Elba, AA/K Paterson; **134/135** Palazzo dei Consoli, Gubbio, AA/T Harris; **136** Orvieto, AA/K Paterson; **136/137** Leaning Tower of Pisa, AA/C Sawyer; **138 & 138/139** San Gimignano, AA/K Paterson; **140** Siena, AA/C Sawyer; **140/141** Duomo, Siena, AA/T Harris; **141** Campello San Clitunno, Spoleto, AA/K Paterson; **142** Urbino, AA/T Souter; **142/143** Todi, AA/K Paterson; **143** Volterra, Roman Ruins, AA/R Ireland; **149** Ostia Antica, AA/C Sawyer; **150** Bocca del Verita, AA/J Holmes; **150/151** Statues of Castor and Pollox, AA/A Kouprianoff; **152** Ponte Sant'Angelo, AA/S McBride; **152/153** Galleria Borghese, AA/D Miterdiri; **153** Palazzo Altemps, AA/S McBride; **154** Palazzo Barberini, AA/P Wilson; **154/155** Palazzo Doria, AA/P Wilson; **156** Fontana di Trevi, AA/S McBride; **156/157** Spanish Steps, AA/C Sawyer; **158** San Clemente, AA/S McBride; **159t** San Giovanni in Laterno, AA/S McBride; **159c** Santa Maria Maggiore, AA/S McBride; **160/161** Market, L'Aquila, AA/C Sawyer; **162/163** Amphitheatre, Ostia Antica, AA/S McBride; **163** Villa Adriana, Tivoli, AA/S McBride; **169** Costa Smeralda, Sardinia, AA/C Sawyer; **170** Castel Nuovo, Naples, AA/M Jourdan; **170/171** Palazzo Reale, Naples, AA/M Jourdan; **171** Castle Sant Elmo, Naples, AA/M Jourdan; **172/173** Capodimonte Gardens, Naples, AA/M Jourdan; **174** Wine bottles, AA/T Souter; **174/175** Bari, AA/C Sawyer; **175** Basilica di San Nicola, Bari, AA/C Sawyer; **176/177** Santa Maria del Isola, Tropea, AA/T Souter; **177** Castel del Monte, Puglia, AA/C Sawyer; **178/179** Sasso Caveoso, AA/T Souter; **179** Paestum, AA/T Souter; **180** Reggio, AA/C Sawyer; **180/181** Costa Smeralda, AA/C Sawyer; **182/183** Mount Etna, Taormina, AA/C Sawyer; **183** Cefalu, AA/C Sawyer

Every effort has been made to trace the copyright holders, and we apologise in advance for any accidental errors. We would be happy to apply the corrections in the following edition of this publication.